# Glassbead Books
John Holbo, Editor

# Reading Graphs, Maps, Trees

## Responses to Franco Moretti

Edited by Jonathan Goodwin & John Holbo

a Valve book event

Parlor Press
Anderson, South Carolina
www.parlorpress.com

Parlor Press LLC, Anderson, South Carolina, 29621
Printed in the United States of America
© 2011 by Parlor Press.

SAN: 254-8879

Library of Congress Cataloging-in-Publication Data

Reading Graphs, maps & trees : responses to Franco Moretti / edited by Jonathan Goodwin & John Holbo.
    p. cm.
"A Valve Book event."
Includes bibliographical references.
ISBN 978-1-60235-205-6 (pbk. : alk. paper) -- ISBN 978-1-60235-206-3 (Adobe ebook)
1. Moretti, Franco, 1950- Graphs, maps, trees. 2. Fiction--History and criticism. 3. Literature--Philosophy. 4. Criticism. I. Goodwin, Jonathan, 1973 Nov. 26- II. Holbo, John, 1967- III. Title: Reading Graphs, maps and trees.
PN3331.M6737 2011
809--dc22
                            2010054541

The book you are holding—if you are holding a book—is available as a free PDF download. Visit http://www.parlorpress.com

Parlor Press, LLC is an independent publisher of scholarly and trade titles in print and multimedia formats. This book is available in paper and Adobe eBook formats from Parlor Press on the World Wide Web at http://www.parlorpress.com or through online and brick-and mortar bookstores. For submission information or to find out about Parlor Press publications, write to Parlor Press, 3015 Brackenberry Drive, Anderson, South Carolina, 29621, or email editor@parlorpress.com.

Cover design Belle Waring.

Franco Moretti's *Graphs, Maps, Trees: Abstract Models For Literary History* is published by Verso (2005).

This 'book event' consisted of a series of posts about Moretti's book at THE VALVE. The event was organized by Jonathan Goodwin. Readers met author, semi-seminar-style; still more readers left comments, blog-style. For this book, the posts have been edited for typos, clarity, style, second thoughts, suitability for inclusion. The original event archive as a whole has a permanent URL, should you wish to compare the original versions of these pieces with the versions included here:

http://www.thevalve.org/go/valve/archive_asc/C48/

Paper has been a bit of a puzzle. We have opted to make it typographically clear where links appear in the electronic version. Readers of the paper version who wish to follow links can download the PDF version of the book from Parlor Press, or check the original posts.

# contents

# Contents

# ◖introduction

**Jonathan Goodwin**

There was almost universal enthusiasm for the perceived novelty and brilliance of Franco Moretti's project in our book event, the third such event the Valve has hosted. Inter- and multi-disciplinarity is both praised and reviled by many academics; there is a sense that traditional disciplines are outmoded administrative conveniences but also suspicion of the possibility of mastering another field in an era of hyper-specialization. As a way of helping to assess this phenomenon in literary history and criticism, I will briefly discuss the use of interdisciplinary techniques in Moretti's previous work, with special attention to the concepts borrowed from evolutionary biology. Afterwards, I will give an overview of the contributions in the present volume, many of which take as their starting point Moretti's interest in evolution.

Purchasers of the most recent edition of Moretti's collection of essays, *Signs Taken for Wonders*, may have noticed that the essay "On Literary Evolution" was not included. According to Moretti, this was an oversight. I mention this because many of the ideas that would lead to *GMT* are first presented here, and I wondered briefly if it were deliberately left out of the collection due to obsolescence. Moretti uses an evolutionary metaphor at the beginning of the essay. He argues that a Lamarckian understanding of evolution, one where variations are goal-oriented, characterizes the understanding of culture and of theories of history derived from Hegel. He suggests that instead it might be useful to apply a Darwinian understanding to this aspect of cultural evolution: what if variations in literary history are not teleological, and to explore the consequences of this postulate.

Moretti proposes first that chance generates rhetorical variations in literary history, with social necessity then selecting some of these variations (263). He borrows from Gould and Eldredge's concept of punctuated equilibrium to describe the "long periods of boredom, short periods of terror" (268) in the development of literary forms. Hans Robert Jauss's account of the success of the literary work being proportional to its distance from the age's horizon of expectations is, for Moretti, essentially monistic.

The Italian critic Francesco Orlando's concept of "figurality rate," which Moretti closely identifies with literary complexity, provides a means of evaluating the micro-historical literary evolution process. (Moretti also uses some ideas about complexity theory from Prigogine and Stengers here to suggest the non-predictability of rapid conceptual change in the historical process.) The startling claim that follows is that the density of modernist poetry, with its never-before-equaled figurality rate, arises as an exaptation (in Gould and Vrba's sense, the use of a trait or the combination of traits out of contingency rather than as a selected-for adaptation) from the development of ambiguity in the monologue in the tragic plot.

Moretti's next work, *The Way of the World, The Bildungsroman in European Culture*, mentions the realization he had about the Russian Formalists' critical novelty after reading Gould and Eldredge (247 n11) and also deploys the punctuated equilibrium concept to describe rapid conceptual change (232). The essay, "A Useless Longing for Myself. The Crisis of the European Bildungsroman, 1898-1914" also specifically invokes the punctuated equilibrium metaphor. I mention this because it leads to one of the key observations that underlies *GMT* and was explicitly developed in work beginning with "Conjectures on World Literature" and "The Slaughterhouse of Literature" in addition to *Atlas of the European Novel, 1800-1900*: that the canon is very small. Therefore, the new forms that develop and drive literary evolution emerge out of long periods of non-canonical stasis and lack of differentiation.

The change in Moretti's project that begins around *The Atlas of the European Novel* depends on the realization that, while the canonical texts are the bottlenecks of literary evolution, that they cannot be studied in isolation. He humorously describes close reading as a "secularized theology" emanating from New Haven ("Slaughterhouse" 208), and suggests that, to understood world literature in its context, that "distant reading" has to replace it ("Conjectures" 56). The great unread mass must be studied in order to see macroevolutionary patterns in literary history. The canonical texts are those which persist from generation-to-generation. They have the ability, even if they are not immediately popular, to entice readers to discover their virtues. (Moretti describes a similar dynamic with the worldwide reaction to the Hollywood film in "Planet Hollywood.") In a footnote, Moretti mentions that both *The Red and the Black* and *Moby Dick*, two conventional counterexamples, went through many editions in the era when they are claimed to have been ignored or unappreciated ("Slaughterhouse" 210 n4).

Contributor to this volume Cosma Shalizi wrote a useful review of *Atlas of the European Novel, 1800-1900* in which he took Moretti to task for some failure to use all of the statistical tools at his disposal. He found Moretti's project interesting enough to review however, and he is a statistical physicist by trade. I will discuss Shalizi's ideas about Moretti in more detail a bit later, but I bring this up to highlight the self-conscious novelty of Moretti's scientific approach. Critics might, and I believe have, called it "scientistic," an insult as deadly as "positivist" in literary studies. Though I do not agree with this assessment, I feel that the abstract and scientific basis ("a more rational literary history") is so central to Moretti's project that it should be discussed.

Shalizi tweaks some humanistic noses a bit in his review, noting that Moretti is able to quote from the popular writings of Darwin and Kuhn's *Structure* intelligently, leaving the reader to infer that this is rare. As we have seen, Moretti's range of reference to evolutionary biology is heavily inclined toward Gould, and the ideas of exaptation and punctuated equilibrium do transfer well to literary studies. (In one of his responses in this volume, Moretti notes that he is not impressed with many of the current efforts in literary studies to use evolutionary approaches. Most of these have been strongly influenced by strains of evolutionary psychology, and Gould's polemic against that, and, in the larger context, the strong adaptationism of Dawkins and Dennett, seems to have influenced him as well.) As the foreword to *GMT* notes, Moretti was trained in a Marxist tradition that emphasized the scientific search for truth and objectivity and reacted against the discipline's turn to French and German metaphysics (2).

Alberto Piazza, one of the authors of *The Human Geography of Genes*, writes an afterword to *GMT* which discusses the potential usefulness of evolutionary concepts in literary studies from the perspective of a population geneticist. Piazza identifies genetic drift as an important concept in cultural transmission which would need further elaboration in Moretti's model (104). Piazza notes the the phylogenetic tree in molecular biology presupposes no natural selection effects, since the convergences and divergences exhibited by selective pressure would cancel each other out, but that the trees devised by Moretti are primarily interested in the selected-for effects. (Piazza also notes the presence of Mayr's allopatric speciation in Moretti's work on the spread of free indirect style, another major evolutionary theoretical concept used to illustrate a pattern in literary history.) The use of phylogenetic trees in evolutionary biology, according to Piazza, is best suited to the history of a gene. The autonomous aspects of the unit in question in Moretti's literary analysis and how it can be compared to the biological concept of a gene is discussed briefly in my contribution to this volume.

Before turning to an overview of this volume's contents, I will briefly review the illuminating exchange between Moretti and Christopher Prendergast in the *New Left Review* on *GMT*. Prendergast argues that Moretti does not have a causal mechanism to explain why readers of Arthur Conan Doyle selected "clues" as the main determinant of his popularity, and Moretti answers that, while he did propose a black box type of mechanism here, he now believes that cognitive science might provide an explanatory mechanism (75), it's worth noting that Moretti cites Steven Johnson's entry in this volume—and personal communication resulting from it, as the source of this insight). The major theoretical problem that Prendergast identifies in *GMT* is that Moretti posits a divergent model of cultural evolution whereas the presiding explanations for models of cultural change emphasize convergence. The persistence of symbolic forms, for Moretti, is why literary history branches rather than amalgamates.

A recurrent point in Moretti's response to Prendergast is the distinction proposed by Noam Chomsky between problems and mysteries. Problems have a field of conceptual understanding; not everything is known but the contours of inquiry are well-established. Progress has been charted and will continue. Mysteries, on the other hand, are not understood. Progress has not been made on them, though their formulation dates to antiquity. Moretti ends his response by noting that the concepts he has addressed in *GMT* are largely mysteries, whereas Prendergast's specific criticisms suggest that they are problems. The abstractional techniques are exploratory measures designed to reduce mysteries to problems, as Chomsky has described his work in linguistics.

Moretti concludes with a reconsideration of the liberatory or demystifying potential of his project, an aspect of his work important since his Marxist formation.

I will now review how the essays in this volume deal with the challenges Moretti makes to literary history. John Holbo begins his entry by observing that literary scholarship is not entirely cumulative. For Holbo, literary scholars have a culture of ignoring each other's arguments and "results," such as they are, and operate in a type of hermetic isolation. The comments to Holbo's post pressed him on this point, with "CR," an assistant professor, describing his experiences having his articles rejected because they did not do enough of just what Holbo had said literary scholars never do: cite other people's work and place theirs in the larger context. The miscommunication here seemed based on a different methodological understanding: from John Holbo's perspective in philosophy and his concurrent interest in the philosophical basis of literary theory in the Continental tradition, the narrowing of a problem-set based on successive attempts seems a definingly absent trend in literary studies. From CR's perspective, the almost ritualistic obeisance required to a "methodology" or tradition of readings of a given text is itself stifling.

Ray Davis criticizes Moretti for what seem to be surprising conceptual omissions: philosophy and cognitive science. As we have seen, Moretti does agree about the importance of mental models for understanding the evolution of literary forms. And, though it is specifically the French/German metaphysical tradition that Moretti is reluctant to engage, it is interesting to consider to what extent writers in that tradition could illuminate his project.

Matthew Kirschenbaum describes what was known as the 'nora project', which is now known as the 'monk project'. Kirschenbaum's entry deals mostly with the project's digital humanities and data mining initatives and only tangentially with Moretti's work. At the same time, however, it is arguably the most relevant entry to the future of what Moretti proposes here because of the role digitization and database searches will play in the next generation of "distant readings." (Moretti's "The Novel: History and Theory" contains the following: "With digital databases, this is now easy to imagine: a few years, and we'll be able to search just about all novels that have ever been published, and look for patterns among billions of sentences" (114), for example.) With the automatic searching and identifying of generic features, the production and analysis of the data similar to what Moretti does in *GMT* will be able to happen with much larger sample sizes and, therefore, much greater accuracy. Some generic features are obviously more subject to automated recognition than others. Free indirect style, for instance, is easier to recognize than "clues."

Timothy Burke makes a number of wide-ranging observations in his essay. He draws on his experience as an Africanist historian to note that even what makes its way in the archive, vast as it is, is still only a small sample of the total number of cultural objects in circulation. (Presumably it's a large enough sample that statistical inferences from it can be made, but the point about it being a sample is clearly important here.) Curiously enough, Burke suggests that Moretti has too gradualist an approach to evolutionary metaphors, which suggests that even a writer as enamored of the punctuated metaphors as Moretti can be criticized by a cultural historian impressed with the power of the idea. Burke also argues that Moretti should be more interested in complexity theory and emergence, a topic which does show up in the "On Literary Evolution" essay from *Signs Taken for Wonders*. But more attention to what is clearly an important analytic problem is needed for the long-term viability of Moretti's project. (Piazza's afterword notes the severe problems introduced into quantitative analysis by disturbingly common non-linear processes.)

Adam Roberts, inspired by the generational model of genre development in *GMT*, outlines a generic history of science fiction in the next article. Based largely on his *The History of Science Fiction*, Roberts proposes a development of successive genres since Kepler's *Somnium* and suggests that they would follow a pattern, if graphed, similar to that of Figure 9 of *GMT*, "British Novelistic Genres, 1740-1900" (19). The difficulty in both of these graphs is disagreement about the morphology of the genres, as both Moretti and Roberts note. Bill Benzon then raises the issue of cognitive maps and where they fit in with Moretti's geographical ones. I found this to be a particularly interesting issue, especially given Moretti's theoretical background. Benzon raises the quite interesting point about what degree of geographical accuracy could be expected from the authors of the various novels Moretti lists. He cites a Donald Norman experiment where graduate students could not accurately map the apartments they lived in while they were in those apartments, yet they presumably never had trouble navigating them. The distance between the cognitive map and the unconscious understanding of the environment is another issue where research in cognitive science could supplement Moretti's research aims.

Eric Hayot's piece is the first to address the academic sociology of Moretti's project. As he describes, there is both considerable joy at the novelty and deep suspicion at not just the perceived scientism but also the attitude that the "secular theology" of close reading has been blasphemed against. Hayot uses Lindsay Waters' argument against the elimination of joy and the erotics of reading in modern hermeneutics as polar opposite of Moretti's work. Hayot is not so willing to dismiss either explicitly or tacitly the status quo as most of our contributors seem to do, at least for the purposes of evaluating Moretti's argument, and his contribution is salutary in that regard, especially for reminding us just how radical and how much of an outsider project this is. My brief essay attempts to examine what, if anything, the concept of the "ideologeme" adds to Moretti's theoretical framework. Coming as it does with a rich Marxian pedigree, I suggest that "ideologemes," if adequately defined, would serves as a useful analogy to the suspicious "memes" of sociobiology.

I noted earlier that Moretti quoted Steven Berlin Johnson's contribution in his response to Prendergast in the *NLR*. Johnson's point about needing a plausible psychological model to explain formal invention and reception was identified as an important area for future research. It is where my own interests in Moretti's project mostly lie, and one of the reasons that I was initially drawn to Moretti's work. In the comments to Johnson's entry, both Bill Benzon and Ray Davis elaborate on the need for a psychological theory of aesthetics, one that takes into account scientific research and that does not, as Davis points out, rely too heavily on facile generalization. It is a hard problem, and I find the appearance of it in the discussion of a book that's resolutely sociological in its focus to be interesting and refereshing.

Jenny Davidson criticizes Moretti for failing to recognize the points of contact between his own project and the feminist tradition of recovery, especially insofar as many of the same texts and periods are covered by both. Much of Moretti's work tries to establish the basis for canon formation, not critique it as such. Davidson usefully refers to other work whose scope and aims are similar to Moretti's: Wai Chee Dimock's two articles, "Planetary Time and Global Translation: 'Context' in Literary Studies" and "Genre as World System: Epic and Novel on Four Continents," are both, especially in their deployment of self-similarity in what Davidson calls a response to historicism, especially illuminating in this regard. In a challenge to Moretti's emphasis on divergence in cultural evolution, Davidson claims that contingency has been widely accepted as a facet of culture. In the Marxian tradition, however, teleology is far more important than contingency and might even have been considered heretical at times. The importance of contingency as a role in cultural evolution and historical understanding is a popular subject certainly; witness the long-standing tradition of alternative history writing. But I agree with Moretti that the emphasis on contingency and variation as a generative principle is in fact contrary to the dominant models of cultural and literary history.

John Holbo's second post raises the exciting theoretical question of marketing. The influence of advertising on the spread of formal devices does seem to be, as Holbo claims, an elided aspect of Moretti's analysis. Particularly now, when the statistical sophistication and database extensiveness of the modern marketing industry has exceeded even the most utopian proto-fantasies of a Leopold Bloom, the question of how markets are malleable through indirect interference and manipulation seems crucial. Moretti's work on the Hollywood film does seem to suggest that it is the genre or the formal aspects of film itself which create its market. The words "advertising" and "marketing" do not appear in "Planet Hollywood," for instance. Holbo reintroduces "dumb luck" into the equation with the inexplicably huge success of J. K. Rowling. Davidson notes in the comments that Rowling's work seesa simply not as good (formally inventive, complex, satisfying) as that of at least some of her peers, so some regression to the mean of popular taste would have to be a factor. She also claims that this is not the case with Doyle; compared to his peers, he is a better, more complex writer, a claim which Moretti's analysis would seem to support. In his response to this round of inquiries, Moretti invokes a principle from the study of dynamic non-linear systems: that there must be a small initial difference in morphology of form that accounts for the large-scale change in magnitude seen in the market results.

Sean McCann begins by making the same observation that Jenny Davidson did: that Moretti is a singular figure in literary studies who will inspire no school of research because of several factors, the most important of which is that only he is capable of doing these kinds of projects in a way that holds others' interests. Though I disagree with this claim, I recognize its force. Prendergast makes a similar observation in his long response to *GMT*. If it were not for Moretti's unique theoretical trajectory, coming as he does from a background in Marxist aesthetics, the project would immediately recall a sterile positivist approach associated by Prendergast with Gustave Lanson (43), in particular. McCann identifies two environments of Moretti's analysis: the market and the mental. According to McCann, Moretti's market environment requires a different selection agent than the social environment, so the evolutionary analogy between them needs further development Here again is another instance in which a cognitive scientific approach would advance the ideas found in *GMT*. I also think that Moretti would not as easily accept the distinction between these two types of environments.

This brings us at last to the final and longest essay in the collection, Cosma Shalizi's "Graphs, Trees, Materialism, Fishing." Shalizi begins his essay by noting that Moretti invited him to participate in a seminar on the future of the novel after reading his review of *Atlas of the European Novel*. Cosma Shalizi is, as he himself notes, perhaps the ideal reader of a project like Moretti's, combining statistical expertise with considerable polymathy. In the first section of his essay, Shalizi applies statistical analysis to Moretti's claim that clusters of genre appear and disappear within a generation. He finds that they do, but admonishes Moretti that the point of quantitative data is to enable precise inference, so there is no need to return to intuitive analysis. I do not know the extent to which Moretti consulted a statistician in the writing of *GMT*, but it is a complex discipline whose results famously contradict intuition on occasion. (Moretti does cite Hacking's *The Taming of Chance* several times in earlier work.)

The distinctiveness of each textual unit that makes up a genre and how that fact compares to population biology is next point Shalizi emphasizes. If you classify texts purely according to morphology, then phylogenetic similarity is sacrificed. Does that level of the metaphor extend? This is one of the questions that I asked in my contribution, which started by raising the notion of "memes" or the ideologeme as a constraining unit of cultural heredity (as I have to agree with Prendergast and, presumably, everyone else, that litera-ture does not have *genes* as such). The next point of conten-tion has also been raised by Prendergast in his essay, though Shalizi approaches it from a broader (and more critical) perspective. The Hegelian notion of "expressive totality" (the phrase seems to be Althusser's) and the interpretive problems that result from trying to make complex inferences about the social world from a sample size, often, of one cultural object, disturbs Shalizi. He offers the surprising and useful observation that comparative methods taken from the bio-logical sciences which use lattices capable of modeling such phenomenon as lateral-gene transfer would not depend on the determination of whether or not literature had "discrete-valued, particulate factors, such as genes." As I have written earlier, this question seems to me fundamental in assessing the likely success of Moretti's approach, and I find this type of modeling, as of yet unattempted, to the best of my knowl-edge, to be an exciting opportunity.

Another issue where Shalizi differs from Moretti is in his distinction between the social forces causing a change in taste and those "which shape the *content* of the taste." Shalizi, following Stanley Lieberson's *A Matter of Taste*, suggests that these two forces have to be distinguished and do not always have a determinative relation. Such an idea is deeply anti-thetical to the main tenets of Marxian thought, however, not least of which to the expressive totality and teleology of form that Moretti remains influenced by. One new wrinkle Shalizi provides in the repeated idea seen in many of the entries here that a psychological understanding of formal reception and change is needed is to appeal to the empirical studies done of reading and response. The literature that Shalizi refers to, while certainly noteworthy and interesting in itself, will not readily satisfy many comparatists covering the same literary ground as Moretti because of the vast gulf between the highly aestheticized type of reading they are accustomed and the presumably sterile and artificial experiments that can be studied with empirical methods. (Norm Holland's *5 Readers Reading* is an earlier and useful addition to the list of relevant works that Shalizi mentions here.) Empirical studies of reader-response are also far removed from Moretti's description of close-reading as a secular theology.

Shalizi concludes his essay with the comforting thought that the randomness inherent in human history and cultural products of that history, have, by that very randomness, "strict nonrandom regularity," which can be analyzed using methods such as Moretti's or by the more traditional technique of close reading. That seemingly paradoxical—yet pleasing—idea seems as good as place as any to conclude this introduction. I do want to mention that the comments made throughout the book event were unusually substantive and provocative. Please browse around in the archive, no matter how you happen to be reading.

### Works Cited

Dimock, Wai Chee. "Genre as World System: Epic and Novel on Four Continents." *Narrative* 14.1 (2006): 85-101.

—. "Planetary Time and Global Translation: 'Context' in Literary Studies." *Common Knowledge* 9.3 (2003): 488-507.

Moretti, Franco. *Atlas of the European Novel, 1800-1900*. Verso, 1998.

— "Conjectures on World Literature." *NLR* 1 (Jan-Feb 2000): 54-68.

—. "The End of the Beginning." *NLR* 41 (Sept-Oct 2006): 71-86.

—. *Graphs, Maps, Trees: Abstract Models for Literary History*. Verso, 2005.

—. "The Novel: History and Theory." *NLR* 52 (July-Aug 2008): 111-124.

—. "Planet Hollywood." *New Left Review* 9 (May-Jun 2001): 90-101.

—. "The Slaughterhouse of Literature." *Modern Language Quarterly* 61.1 (2000): 207-227.

—. *Signs Taken for Wonders*. 2nd ed. London: Verso, 1987.

—. "A Useless Longing for Myself. The Crisis of the European Bildungsroman, 1898-1914." Ralph Cohen, ed. *Studies in Historical Change*. Charlottesville, U of Virginia Press, 1992. 43-59.

—. *The Way of The World: The Bildundgsroman in European Culture*. Verso, 2000.

Prendergast, Christopher. "Evolution and Literary History." *New Left Review* 34 (July-Aug 2005): 40-62.

Roberts, Adam. *The History of Science Fiction*. Palgrave, 2006.

Shalizi, Cosma. "One Effort More, Litterateurs, if You Would Be Empiricists!" Review of *Atlas of the European Novel*. 21 (Oct 1998. 28 Nov 2008). http://www.cscs.umich.edu/~crshalizi/reviews/atlas-of-the-european-novel/.

# Reading Graphs, Maps, Trees

## Responses to Franco Moretti

# ① Graphs, Maps, Trees, Fruits of The MLA

**JOHN HOLBO**

Moretti opens "Graphs" by remarking,

> what a minimal fraction of the literary field we all
> work on: a canon of two hundred novels, for instance,
> sounds very large for nineteenth-century Britain
> (and is much larger than the current one), but is still
> less than one per cent of the novels that were actually
> published: twenty thousand, thirty, more, no one
> really knows—and close reading won't help here, a
> novel a day every day of the year would take a century
> or so.

This reminds me of a point made in MY INAUGURAL
VALVE POST. How many members in the MLA? The large
number is largely a function of the number of college courses
that need teaching, freshman essays that need marking, not
really at all a function of any independent conception of a humanistic knowledge edifice that needs approximately twenty
or thirty thousand toiling professorial hands—obliged to
produce, yes even *over*-produce. Call this dynamic of su-
perfluity 'sorcerer's apprentice syndrome'. It's not the worst
problem, but it deserves address from every promising angle.
Moretti's project presents a fresh angle: an institutionally vast
discipline should try to find projects suitable for pursuit by
vast numbers of scholars. Actually existing academic literary studies makes considerably more sense *if* something like

◀ 3

Moretti's project makes sense. So, on behalf of the institution, there should be a concerted effort to make sense of such projects. Which is no guarantee sense can be made. (Nor am I proposing all English professors be conscripted as Moretti's research assistants. No, not at all.)

Let me make the same point a different way (anticipating and answering an objection.) In his second paragraph Moretti lists a number of scholars on whose work he builds. "I mention these names right away because quantitative work is truly cooperation: not only in the pragmatic sense that it takes forever to gather the data, but because such data are ideally independent from any individual researcher, and can thus be shared by others, and combined in more than one way." Examples follow: graphs charting the take-off of the novel in Britain, Japan, Italy, Spain and Nigeria; data amounting to knowledge that could not plausibly be approximated by anything in an intuitive, appreciative head—however prodigiously well-read: an Easter Island-style monument. Like Harold Bloom, say.

But now the inevitable objection: to suggest that literary studies take the quantitative turn is preposterous, Gradgrindian positivism. I am sure Moretti gets this a lot, so he surely has his answer down pat, but I'll make one on his behalf (which is therefore not necessarily his.) Just as we are accustomed to the existence of a standing army of academic literary critics, so that we should be pinched from time to time, to wake up to how strange this institution is—how obscure in its actual, aggregate intellectual (as opposed to pedagogic) function. I think we are overly accustomed to the profound *lack* of cooperation that is the hallmark of humanities research. We could use occasional reminders of this very fact. Most literary scholars would no more simply *use* the 'results' of a fellow scholar than they would use her toothbrush (I heard that joke somewhere.) Not without first transforming, interrogating, refashioning so that this implement is made the new possessor's own. To look at a shelf of journals and see, mostly, rows of used toothbrushes, is not an energizing prospect, however.

I don't mean to be apocalyptic about it. It's a peculiar situation, not the Downfall of Western Civilization. I also don't mean to suggest the problem is unique to English professors. (I think the original toothbrush joke was about professors generally, or maybe it was even about scientists.) But the problem is as acute in literary studies as anywhere, so it may as well be addressed here. I am personally in a position to say it is less severe in philosophy departments, where there is more consensus about what counts as an argument, hence more neutral portability of certain products. But, of course, portability does not automatically equate to intellectual value. Perhaps the philosophy department has purchased communication at the cost of significance, declining into a sort of puzzle-piece scholasticism, which likes to pretend it is brick-on-brick scientism. But scholasticism is at least a presumptively seemly ethos for *scholars*. That is *something*. Given the fact that there are so many scholars, they ought to be seeking ways to make themselves more ... scholastic—while fending off decline into empty scholasticism, yes of course we need that, too.

Obviously this is going to be a pendulum thing. Too many Morettis will call forth a new Edmund Wilson, making fun of "The Fruits of the MLA," which will not be funny paper titles this time around, but mindlessly headlong factual accretions—graphs, maps and trees of no conceivable interest to anyone, save those so inclined to the ceremonial overproduction of graphs, maps and trees that they miss the forest of hermeneutic/aesthetic interest. (Do people recall that Wilson wrote an MLA-mocking piece in 1968, complaining about the excesses of the MLA? But these alleged excesses were utterly unlike the alleged excesses we associate with the journalistic genre of MLA mockery in the 1980's and 90's. Things change, while staying the same.)

But it seems to me the problem of too many Morettis is yet to arise, and should be dealt with if it does, not pre-emptively. Because, to repeat, this is one of those pendulum swing things.

It seems to me, to repeat, that the oddity of the deep incommunicability of results, within a large academic discipline—the lack of portability of the products across vast fields and subfields—should strike us more than it tends to. If it did, we would welcome projects lke Moretti's more eagerly. An institution should look to its nature, try to find things that it is suited to do (as well as trying to change its nature so as to be capable of things it presently isn't suited to do well, yes of course.) So again: actually existing academic literary studies makes more sense *if* something like Moretti's project makes sense.

The next objection strikes like clockwork: but you can't just demand that literary studies professors start accepting each other's results the way math professors accept each other's proofs. The toothbrush joke suggests an arbitrary fastidiousness. It sounds as if I am saying scholars *could* just accept each other's results but they *won't*. But the hermeneutic character of the humanistic enterprise (characterize it how you like) means this is more a case of *can't* than *won't*. Well, yes. But as an objection to what I am saying this has traction only if the likes of Moretti are not just quantifiers but mono-maniac deniers of the possibility of anything valuable slipping through their nets of number. Which he isn't. The final two sentences of section 1 of the first essay. "A more rational literary history. That's the idea." Not a *totally* Rational history, goodness no.

Why rationalize history? Well, because we *can*, would be argument one. And it is Moretti's. Because literary studies is less well off if we *can't* would be argument 2, which I have made. I feel odd even making it, because it seems so obvious. Is it obvious to you?

## Postscript

Comments to this post were good and useful. There was also sharp disagreement, and it became clear to me what I wrote was doomed to be misunderstood in certain ways. Let me append a few post-thoughts that amount to clarifications of what I meant to say. (I also encourage readers who find this interesting to read all the old comments. But I'm not going to rehash them.)

For about a year after I wrote this post it seemed to me literary scholars I bumped into, attended conferences with, or corresponded with, were buzzing about Moretti, quite independently of our little event. He seemed to be enjoying a moment of academic celebrity. Fine by me. But it surprised me how much of the buzz was negative. I was struck, in particular, by one panel discussion I attended (yes, an MLA panel) at which it was more or less agreed by various participants that scholarship and pedagogy of literary history are, at present, mutually ill-suited. (I am providing my own gloss on their agreement, if memory serves. But I'll withhold names, in case memory does not serve. Maybe this is just me talking to myself here.) On the one hand, you need a set of texts that will provide you with sufficient evidence to pronounce intelligently—justifiably—on such subjects as 'the nineteenth century American novel'. On the other hand, you need a set of texts to fill out a 12-16 week syllabus for an undergraduate course of that title. There isn't any one set of texts that can do both jobs.

Of course it isn't so surprising that the most sophisti-cated scholarship goes beyond what can be crammed into a single undergraduate semester. But there is more to the point. There seems to be a tendency for *good* undergraduate peda-gogy to recapitulate *bad* (as opposed to merely incomplete or preliminary) historiography. The teacher finds herself proceeding as if 'the nineteenth century novel' (pick your suitably broad subject) is the sort of thing that is at all likely to show up through the lens of eight novels to be read. The truth is: reading a small number of novels and writing a few interpretive essays can be a fine and enriching way to spend a few months. But it's not the same *kind* of enriching activity as studying the novel historically, with scholarly rigor. And no one really thinks otherwise. So tension between pedagogy and historiography is not just tension between for-students simplification and for-scholars sophistication. It is tension between value and validity. You are asking people to use one method—close reading—to arrive at answers that re-quire a different method—distant reading (to use Moretti's term.)The value of literature is substantially derived from close reading activity (broadly conceived—you can be more hermeneutic or erotic about these virtues of closeness, as you like.) But many sorts of scholarly claims demand more 'dis-tant reading' methods, on pain of invalidity. So how do you proceed, if value and validity tug against each other, rather than going together, as one would have wished?

Sitting in the audience at this panel, thinking my own way through all this, I was innocently waiting for someone to point out that Moretti might help. Yet three out of four of the scholars on this panel were *very* negative about Moretti when his name (inevitably) came up. They were almost (not quite) dismissive. The fourth seemed impressed mostly by the new-ness of Moretti's project; seemed heartened that there was a new thing some scholars were enthusiastic about. But surely there is more to be enthusiastic here than enthusiasm itself.

Let me put the point yet another way. Rereading the contributions to our event, I am struck by contrasts between respondents who were otherwise in basic agreement. I say Moretti is good because he is imitable. Sean McCann approves of Moretti, but predicts he will be largely un-imitable. Tim Burke writes: "Of all the odd things I've heard in recent years, one of the oddest would be that there are objections in principle to the research paradigm that Franco Moretti describes in *Graphs, Maps, Trees*." But Jenny Davidson quotes Elif Batuman regarding Moretti's "irresistible magnetism of the diabolical." She says she is "at once seduced and rendered wary" by this distinctive quality, which she associates with the 'heresy' of quantification. How is it possible that an author can seem, at once, moderate and agreeable to the point of utter, ecumenical unobjectionablility, yet also 'diabolical', 'heretical'?

If the answer is that literary scholars take the undesirability of quantification for granted, whereas everyone else takes its desirability for granted, the literary folks are flat out of luck. Everyone else is *right*. But I'm quite sure that's not the whole story. (I hope it's not even a significant part of it.)

I think these divergent responses are largely due to divergent ways of taking rather characteristic "grand flourishes" (Davidson's term) Moretti makes on his own behalf. Davidson objects, rather mildly, that Moretti poses as a revolutionary, but seems to be reinventing the wheel. "As a scholar working in the field of eighteenth-century British literature and culture, I find Moretti's work around these questions fruitful but its distinctiveness or originality somewhat overstated. You don't have to be a heroic scientific pioneer and experimentalist to uncover the patterns in long-forgotten British novels of the eighteenth and nineteenth centuries."

Let's consider: 'Distinctiveness or originality somewhat overstated.' I would have said: *surely* highly distinctive even if the *conclusions* are not so original. Moretti's methods will mostly help by acting as an independent check on what we think we already know. And yet: that's very exciting and new. Davidson continues: "Ruth Perry's recent *Novel Relations*, for instance, reaps the rewards of a lifetime of reading eighteenth-century fiction to discern patterns (the rise of the novel of the second attachment, the trope of the *cri de sang*) that are as illuminating as Moretti's graphs about literary and social history." But the concern is obviously going to be that a lifetime spent reading such-and-such a body of material may, after all, reap the reward of a distorted view. (It's not as though we think we know that riding a hobby-horse for years conveys immunity to eccentricity.) Should I trust what Perry has to say or not? If some sort of independent, quantitative confirmation or disconfirmation were possible, that would be extremely welcome. (Confirmation is a more inductively problematic relationship than disconfirmation. Still, if the same result were arrived at by a sensitive critic, reading a body of work, and by a number-cruncher, mining that body of work, that would be confidence-bolstering, if not strictly proof.)

At the time of our event, I think I was more or less reading Moretti's grand flourishes as *just* flourishes. I was enchanted by the humbler possibilities, whereas Davidson was a bit more inclined to take them seriously (the flourishes, that is), hence to regard them as potential hubris. Looking at the text today, I am inclined to split the difference. Partly this is the result of me subsequently coming around to a more skeptical view of many of Moretti's bolder claims. This is *very* important, but too much to shoehorn in here. Let me conclude these afterthoughts the same way I began this piece: by accentuating the positive, in a small way.

It so happens I have just finished reading Jenny Davidson's new book, *Breeding: A Partial History of the Eighteenth Century*. It is a good book, I think. I feel I learned from it. But I am quite sure it is exactly the sort of book that could use Morettiesque methods to *complement* it. There is a tension in Davidson's methodology, and even more so in her characterizations of that methodology. She makes her own problematic gestures of distinctiveness and originality. When we see this, Moretti's humble uses look even more useful.

Here is Davidson's characterization of what is going on in her book: "I wanted, medium-like, to make these pages a sort of parliament, an auditorium in which the voices of actors in and commentators on the story of heredity in the eighteenth century can be heard" (7-8). And: "The great value of this kind of swerve away from the straight-and-narrow of the historical method—what makes it worth the risk—seems to me to lie in the counterfactual or *path-not-taken* traction it offers on ideas" (8). She takes as models W.G. Sebald and Roland Barthes and feels generally confirmed in her faith in, "the writerly approach, an essayistic or discursive mode that prefers not to participate in all of the disciplinary practices of history or criticism proper" (12). Yet, as she writes near the end of the book, "I offer these thoughts in a spirit diametrically opposed to the deliberate amateurism of David Denby's *Great Books: My Adventures With Homer, Rousseau, Woolf, and Other Indestructible Writers of the Western World*. I want to keep all the intensity and the precision of academic writing, and the virtues of specialization, but to make what I write at least potentially open to readers in other disciplines, or in other walks of life" (198).

I think the tension here is fairly obvious: if you are deliberately refusing to fulfill disciplinary expectations; if you are giving up specialization for the serendipitous joys of a swerving, cross-disciplinary jaunt; if you are foregoing a sober, academic style for a more writerly, novelistic one; then whatever makes you better than David Denby can hardly be the fact that you are a properly disciplined, specialized, academic writer, whereas Denby is not. (I have not read Denby and have no opinion whatsoever about the specific case. I really am interested only in the general methodological question.)

And there is another problem here. Davidson's against-the-disciplinary-grain posture is not fully credible because, frankly, this posture *is* the disciplinary grain at the present time. This sort of post-Greenblattian-Auerbachian-Sebaldian-Barthesian, New Historicist, or post-New Historicist 'touch of the real' essayistic-academic style is, if not predominant, then at least very familiar, very commonly met with. It's *normal*. On the one hand, this makes perfect sense: people are attracted to this style for all the reasons Davidson says she is. So they write in this style. But, on the other hand, it *can't* fully make sense for writing against the disciplinary grain to *be* the disciplinary grain.

'Against the grain' feels like automatic, contrarian wisdom; innately in touch with all those confining, facilitating, secure grooves of disciplinarity, specialization, so forth—yet leaping above and beyond all that. Losing touch yet keeping in touch. Inspired yet rigorous. Solidly argued yet boldly leaping. These are the contraries we would *like* to combine. I feel the impulse myself. It's no mystery why people *want* this. But how do we seriously propose to get it? Even harder: how do we suppose that squaring the circle, like that, could be the new disciplinary *normal*. What's the disciplinary *formula* for indulging in counter-disciplinary irregularities on a regular, disciplinary basis?

Moretti is not the guaranteed solution to all such troubles, perhaps not actually the solution to *any* of them. But it seems to me that what should attract writers like Davidson to Moretti, without detracting from their own projects in the least, is the prospect of some *serious* assistance in pulling off these contrary combinations with more conviction. The distinctiveness they achieve hereby may not be so much Moretti's as their own.

Let me put it another way: just as the plural of anecdote is not data, the plural of synecdoche is not historicism. The basic concern about the sort of historicism Davidson practices is that it is argument-by-synecdoche; it persuades by virtue of its essayistic charms. We are given a sample of 'voices'. Very well. How do we know the sample is *valid*? (Read again the passage from Moretti that I started out with.)

I know what Davidson will reply: it's not so easy to approach such a topic in any more systematic way. There's such a hybrid mass of inherently cross-disciplinary, heterogeneous material to come to grips with. (I haven't said anything about Davidson's specific historical claims. Suffice it to say that a study of 18th Century attitudes towards 'breeding' inevitably carries one to many different places.) Fair enough. But that isn't a good reason not to *want* that other thing, let alone to make strictly misleading gestures to the effect that, ordinarily, we *have* that other thing. It is closer to being the exception than the rule.

Were it possible to buttress Davidson's *Breeding* with some bank of Moretti-esque maps, graphs and trees, the latter might just repeat the former, thereby amounting to confirmation (of a not-strictly dispositive sort). But they would still allow Davidson herself to claim, with greater credibility, the sort of distinctiveness she, indeed, wants to claim.

Her style of stroll across the fields is most credible if it truly *is* a break from regular, systematic attempts to survey and plow through those fields. We strengthen—and in no way undermine—the value of 'essayistic' approaches to literary history by encouraging that other sort of approach.

Originally posted January 11, 2006
http://www.thevalve.org/go/valve/article/graphs_maps_trees_fruits_of_the_mla/

## Works Cited

Davidson, Jenny. *Breeding: A Partial History of the Eighteenth Century*. Columbia University Press, 2008.

# ② Graphs, Maps, Trees / Sets Hamper Grasp

**RAY DAVIS**

## I. "Graphs, Maps, Trees" by Franco Moretti

Moretti sounds like a happy guy. And it's infectious. Why pledge allegiance to a groove and turn it into a rut? Get out of that stuffy coffee shop and into a cool refreshing stats lab. Live a little! (With the aid of twenty grad students.) An OuBelLetriPo is overdue. Let's pick a quantitative approach and a subject out of the hat: "Pie charts" and "Coming-out stories"—wait, um, I wasn't ready; can I try again? "Income distribution" and "Aphra Behn"? Perfect!

Will you end up with a demolished bit of received wisdom? A sociological footnote? Or just graphic representation of a critical triteness? *You don't know*! You think Perec knew the plot of *La Disparition* before he started?

From this set of ongoing experiments, "Graphs" seem to be going best. Those cross-cultural Rise-of-the-Novel curves hold immediate appeal.

And what they appeal for is correlation with *something else*. Moretti plausibly and skeptically explains who might've stepped on the brakes when the curve dips, but who revs the engine? Do accelerators vary as inhibitors do?

Even more intriguing is Moretti's report that nineteenth-century English fiction genres tended to turn over in a clump every twenty-five or thirty years, rather than smoothly year by year. But his report relies exclusively on secondary sources, and risks echo chamber artifacts. Are generational timespans a convenience for the researchers he draws from? What if dialogic genres ("Jacobin novel" and "Anti-Jacobin novel") weren't shown separately? How closely do the novel's clumps lock step with transitions in other forms? How far can we reliably carry statistical analysis of a non-random sample of forty-four?

Plenty of intrigue, then, and plenty of opportunity to re-make the mistakes of others who've tried to turn history into a "real science."

Since maps are often referred to by writers (and, when otherwise unavailable, as in fantasy genres, often passed along to the reader), their re-use by critics tends to be confirmatory rather than revelatory—most dramatically when Clive Hart walked each character's path through the "Wandering Rocks" (Hart & Hayman, 181-216). In "Maps," Moretti's diagrams make a good case for a not very startling thesis: a nostalgic series of "village stories" will most likely feature a village from which meanderings are launched but which fades into insignificance over time. As he admits, his scatter plot of Parisian protagonists provides even less novelty: if you have an ambitious young French hero, you start him in the Latin Quarter and aim him elsewhere. (In "The Invention of the Artist's Life," Pierre Bourdieu diagrammed *The Sentimental Education*'s character trajectories on a Parisian map and simi-larly found graphic confirmation of what was never really in doubt.)

Judging by early fruit, "Trees" hold the least promise. As presented, the "free indirect discourse" evolutionary tree doesn't meet Moretti's own standards of rigor, since he offers no material justification for either his selection of source ma-terial or his linkages.

His other evolutionary trees may be most interesting for failing to justify their initiating assumption: that visible decipherable clues define the classic mystery genre. Extending the branches to verifiable examples of "fair play" might draw the tree-builder into unabstractable tangles. In the classic blend of detection with gothic and horror elements, consider how often the resolution seems arbitrary, delivered with a wink. Given how poorly most human beings follow a logical argument, does anything more than lip service *have* to be paid to rationality? To what extent was that expectation set by reviewers rather than noticed by readers? How quickly after the rule's formulation was it challenged by re-assertion of other aspects of crime melodrama in spy stories, thrillers, procedurals, and hard-boiled stories, and then how quickly was it undermined by "cross-breeding"? (My own experience of genre change seems closer to Alfred Kroeber's self-grafting Tree of Human Culture than to species divergence. You only go *so* hardcore before background singers return to the mix.)

More exhaustive and more focused, Moretti's "everything published in the *Strand*" tree carries more conviction (and much less tidiness) than his initial "Conan Doyle and his rivals" tree. Exhaustively constrained to such an extent, though, the tree may describe something less than Moretti seems to hope for. I can imagine a tree tracing certain ingredients of virtual reality stories in 1980s science fiction. But would that graph *evolution* or just Gardner Dozois's editorial obligation to avoid strict repetition?

Moretti closes his trilogy with two general remarks.

One is a call for materialism, eclecticism, and description. This I applaud, since the most interesting scholarship I've read lately includes interdisciplinary studies of "accidentals," histories of readership and publishing, text-crunching of non-canonical sets, whether mechanically or passionately. There's plenty of life even in purely literary anti-interpretive experiments such as those collected in Ben Friedlander's *Simulcast.*

The other "constant" Moretti claims is "a total indifference to the philosophizing that goes by the name of 'Theory' in literature departments." (He doesn't define "Theory" more precisely, but Novalis is apparently not on the prohibited list.) And here, I think, I'll keep my hands quietly folded.

I agree that twentieth century philosophers and psychologists have made awful interpretation factories, and that literary studies sometimes reek of old shit under new labels. But interpretations generated from political science, economics, quantum physics, or fMRI averaging tend to be just as inane. What makes such readings tedious isn't which foreign discipline has been used to slap together a mold, but the inherent moldiness of the affair.

For a critic and pleasure reader like myself, Moretti's text-twice-removed findings fit best in the foundations and framework of aesthetics, clearing false assumptions and blocking overly confident assertions. That's also where neurobiology, developmental and social psychology, and other cognitive sciences seem most useful.

Along with philosophy. Having agreed to open up the field, why ban one of the original players? This isn't the sort of game that's improved by team spirit.

## II. "Sets Hamper Grasp" by A Contrite Form

My interest is really, why do our senses start being filtered? And what does it do to our history and our art?

- BHIKKU 3[1]

—

"Eidetic imagery—the ability to retain in detail a pic-
torial configuration—is found in approximately 8%
of the school population, but almost never in adults,
aside from artists."

In "Senses, Symbols, Operations" (in Perkins), H. Gardner
compared performances of a group of eleven-year-olds and
a group of fourteen-year-olds across a wide variety of per-
ceptual, motor, and cognitive tasks. For the most part, there
was no improvement with age, or there was a slight decline.
Improved: solving brain-teasers; recall of important narrative details. Significantly worse: memory of irrelevant details;
dot-counting.

"... we must ask whether a cultural emphasis on operative thinking has had, as an unintended consequence,
a deleterious effect upon figurative capacities .... the
decline of incidental learning, the waning of interest
in the arts which is so characteristic of adolescence,
and contrasting strategies of adolescents and preadolescents in the style discrimination tasks [adolescents
tending to compare, preadolescents tending to de-
scribe] at least hint at the possibility ..."

—

Even as a schoolboy I took tremendous delight in
Shakespeare, especially the historical plays. I have
also said that formerly pictures gave me considerable
and music very great delight. But now for many years
I cannot endure to read a line of poetry. I have tried
lately to read Shakespeare and found it so intolerably
dull that it nauseated me. I have also lost my taste
for pictures and music .... My mind seems to have

become a kind of machine for grinding general laws
out of large collections of facts but why this should
have caused the atrophy of that part of the brain
alone, on which the higher states depend, I cannot
conceive.

– Charles Darwin

## Afterthoughts

I didn't much like Moretti's book or my review.
Disappointment makes a dull muse; I tried to lend interest
by borrowing Moretti's bluff tone. The result was incoherent: flashy threads on a sketchy character. As punishment,
I was condemned to explain my reaction all over again in
comments.

First I unpacked the reference to "echo chamber artifacts":

> ... there's a post-facto academically-inclined and then
> selectively filtered definition of "genre" being built
> on: it has to be noticeable to late twentieth-century
> Anglo-American literature majors; it can't be too
> short; it can't be too long; then there are the outli-
> ers, like McGann starting modernism with William
> Morris or Aldiss starting science fiction with Mary
> Shelley .... When I've seen people try to delimit living
> "genres," it's been a fiasco, and I'm not sure distance
> clarifies vision. We're not talking chromosome com-
> parisons, or inability to reproduce. Tertiary English
> department results might be like restricting a medical
> research survey to studies financed by pharmaceuti-
> cal companies.

Bill Benzon then pressed me on the perennial topic of cultural evolution.

Some credos:

1. The human species evolved.

2. As a species, humans are inseparably dependent on other humans in ways that go beyond simple repro-duction. We call this dependency "culture." (Note, though, that I haven't personified biological change over time by saying something like "Evolution's goal was culture.")

3. Human beings are attracted to novelty-within-lim-its. The attraction is evidenced both culturally and by studies of individual behavior (insofar as "individual behavior" can be said to exist in a cultural species).

4. The definition of "attractively limited novelty" dif-fers over time, and from individual to individual, and between cultural contexts.

So the desire of the editor to avoid strict repetition com-bines biology (and thus, to some unknowable extent, an "evo-lution" which might be figuratively treated as a motive force), biography, and culture (including a corporate capitalist economy). And, should the editor be successful, that desire could be said to (temporarily) reinforce the cultural expecta-tions that the editor caters to.

What's gained by calling that evolution? Where's the oomph of the metaphor? It may be difficult for biologists to clearly define the limits of "species," but that doesn't begin to compare with the difficulty of defining "sub-genre" or "trend" or "fashion" in a way that can support extended analysis. To say that Dozois' individual choices were an evolutionary force presumes what hasn't yet been proven: that there is "a thing" that evolved from "a different thing" by divergence.

Insofar as a final "thing" could be said to have come out of the virtual reality fad I can only picture it as a set of now-shared assumptions which no longer have to be justified and which are no longer capable of producing a frisson (except among newbies; e.g., academics who'd read no sf and seen no HK movies before *The Matrix* came out.) But such a set would be an example of convergence—a knob in Kroeber's weirdly self-absorbing cultural tree rather than a leaf on Darwin's biological tree.

Even if we jump exclusively to that level of abstraction—sub-genre rather than story—I don't believe we find strict divergence. One of the appeals of VR was its obvious affinity to other meta-narrative techniques/sub-genres; it bolstered itself from the start with borrowings from mystic visions, fairy tales, theater stories, highbrow fourth-wall breaking, and so forth. It could be said to have diverged from some other sf fads of the time, but only by its freedom to re-absorb what had been (temporarily) excluded.

Rather than taking on (and glorying in) all the baggage of "evolution," I'm more inclined to Timothy Burke's imagery of emergence: "dumb luck." I think that's more accurate, less misleading, and—sadly for professional scholars and critics—also much less likely to grab the journalistic imagination.

> ... Given a science fiction scenario in which hybridization was by far the most visible method by which genetic material passed, in which hybridization could happen across almost any examples of any biological species, and in which there was near complete turnover of species every twenty-five to thirty years, do you think that the category of biological species would have developed in any way recognizable to us? Would that world's D4rw1n have explained the origin of species in the same way?

Again, when it comes to literary fashions, marketing, and influence, what (besides confusion) is added by the evolutionary metaphor?

Following Moretti's response, I became increasingly irascible:

All criticism is doomed to analyze only its own perceptions. What the critic is finally saying is, this is my fantasy when faced with the work. What is essential for the interpreter is an ethics of modesty: that he not consider his own perception is the only one.
–"Edgar Allen Poe"
(Friedlander, quoting Rodefer, quoting Kristeva)

Less tentatively than John Emerson, I'm a pluralist. (As a consumer, anyway; as a producer, I'm merely an amateur belletrist.) I enjoy much of the present-day interdisciplinary work which might be classified as "materialist" or "quantitative." And I understand that everyone who works in the humanities considers themselves a member of a beleaguered minority, no matter how successful they might seem to the outside world. But as a pluralist, like John, I feel some need to push back against an either/or tone.

The illusion of rising above one's own time is thrilling, whether the buoyant gas be eternal verities, the universal language of music, or scientific analysis. But history sinks us all eventually, and, despite the earnest (and often well-rewarded) effort put into social and psychiatric sciences, they have a short shelf life. If not many people read Poe's or Twain's or James's criticism nowadays, even fewer build on studies of racial traits and phrenology and hysteria. To paraphrase Prof. Arthur Lee, the social science of today will be the symptom of tomorrow.

*"I may as well admit right away that every time I have studied competition, success, and failure, I have never found that luck played a major role ..."*

That's hardly surprising, since we're not working in controlled laboratory conditions. Explanations can be invented for any event. The problem is proving them. (Disproving proposed explanations, on the hand, is often both doable and worthwhile.) Histories which preclude dumb luck and the strictly unpredictable influence of individuals tend towards the Whiggish or Spenglerian. The excluded arbitrary returns in the form of the historian's decisions.

*"And then again, it may well be that the study of literature will always require, or be enriched by, both close reading and abstraction, interpretations and explanations; but this will amount to saying that literature requires two conceptually opposite approaches. Which is odd, and will make for some interesting speculation on why it should be so."*

As Laura Carroll indicates, "interpretation" is hard to shake free of. For example, Adam Roberts's pre-1900 "science fiction" wouldn't have been analyzable as such until "mainstream realism" became well-enough established to make those isolated works seem like part of a rival tradition. Even choosing what elements to trace through which representatives of a "genre" is an interpretive act, which is why I called the *Strand* spectrum analysis more convincing than the "Conan Doyle's rivals" tree.

Insofar as literature can be said to exist at all, yes, I believe it calls forth both "interpretation" and "explanation"—that is, a desire to narrate the work's intended meaning and a desire to narrate the work's origins. (Already that seems not so binary a opposition.) Or it calls forth a desire to describe the work itself, or to describe our reaction to the work, or, more generally, *to respond*. Trying to pursue all of these approaches at once would, I agree, result in an unholy mess and a shattered career. But that doesn't mean that they're unambiguously opposed.

Let's return to the celebrated clue of the drugged coffee. I haven't read the source story, and so I don't know what its effect in context would be for me, much less for a reader of the time. But I've seen the Continental Op and Philip Marlowe walk more or less knowingly into traps to "shake things up." The detective mystery, broadly defined, shows someone gathering knowledge about criminal circumstances and bringing about an expository conclusion. Presumably drawing from the nearly autistic Holmes, the polite puzzle mystery depicts detached knowledge (represented by the handling of clues, maps, and timetables) and emotional disengagement from the (emotionally arbitrary) conclusion. Hard-boiled mysteries and psychological thrillers, on the other hand, show knowledge as physical experience and insist that observation is inseparable from influence. One might, Moretti-like, try tracing the split by tracking the amount of physical and emotional damage sustained by the detective—beatings in one column, druggings in another—but there would eventually be convergences: Hammett's "drawing room" mystery (set among the detective's dysfunctional friends, with the detective shielded by almost pathological smugness and with a viciously undercut solution); the "Ellery Queen" team's late decision to make Queen a fallible bringer of injustice; Sayers's turn from Wimsey toward Harriet Vane ...

There's not necessarily a conflict between intellectual-emotional engagement and the deployment of evidence. Much of the quantitative, historical, comparative, and materialist research that's been mentioned results in richer or refreshed readings. In that list, I'd include what I've read of Moretti's previous work; on early acquaintance, he sounds like a Marxist Hugh Kenner: a congenial combination. For whatever conscious or unconscious reasons, he seems to have evolved in the direction of Philo Vance, insisting on the need to keep the reading experience (whether current-day or historical) at arm's length. Me, I'm a Black Mask fan. Literature, like murder, is no place for clean hands.

The reception of *Graphs, Maps, Trees* seemed to repeat a familiar irony: confidently self-proclaimed scientific objectivity met by hero-worship, declarations of allegiance, and in-attention to the evidence. By the end of the Valve event, I felt like the hapless (and dickless) EPA inspector of *Ghostbusters*, pointing out the right things in the wrong movie.

As Bob O'Hara summarized in passing, contingent history cannot be made isomorphic with verifiable lab science. Some of this recent rhetoric seems intent on remaking the mistakes of such historical system-builders as Brooks Adams and Oswald Spengler. While scientised literary history will likely contribute to fewer deaths than scientised general history did, it seems even more confused: the aesthetic realm is *defined* by particularity, atemporality, and variation of taste.

Regarding "rigor": If someone vigorously misapplies techniques to rigidly-held arbitrary premises, are the results "rigorous"? They appear so; they even feel so. Still, there's no reason to believe they're true.

An unconsciously developing preference for visible decodable clues "sounds reasonable." But Moretti's clue tree doesn't prove it: the tree never reaches the supposed end goal of evolution; chronological ordering by height is implied but not documented; no evidence is shown that Doyle's rivals at each "level of development" were as popular as Doyle's stories at the same level. The parsimony principle suggests instead that the popularity of the "Sherlock Holmes stories" was due to *Sherlock Holmes*, with visible clues a side-effect of building narratives around such a character: the magician is more effective when audience members inspect the box. What defines a MOR-generic detective novel isn't the quality of its puzzle but the presence of a trademark detective.

But then we're back to personal names, which aren't nearly as scientistic as abstractions.

Sullen bastard that I am, I'm not even cheered up by Steven Berlin Johnson's call for equally "rigorous" use of brain studies.

We've heard what professional philosophers think of the English department's use of philosophy, what mathematicians think of English department Gödel and chaos, and what physicists think of English department entropy and quantum theory. And we've heard some of what professional biologists and cognitive scientists think of "Evolutionary Psychology." Popularized metaphorically applied science is not science. But it is what consumers want, and it's lucrative.

Since 1993, I've been fascinated by application of the cognitive sciences to aesthetics. Since 1995 or so, people who find this out have asked me what I thought of some best-selling book or newspaper article. And I've always had to say that I prefer reading in the primary disciplines. Outside them, we seem to get Just So stories which justify a conservative canon, New Age vapidity, or pop culture tautology. ("People really do enjoy what they seem to enjoy. EEGs prove it!") Working scientists who venture into criticism fare little better. Vilayanur S. Ramachandran's defense of this Chola bronze[2] sounds like a Jungian art appreciation class. If he's describing biologically determined reactions, why does his audience have to be won over? I'd say it's because aesthetics is too complex and socially-personally contingent to support the sort of argument he's making.

Unless we burn art, it outlives our theories about art. I believe the cognitive sciences, cross-cultural history, and philosophy can all shed light on why that is. But where's the percentage? What sells is a familiar story with a twist. 100 newspapers and NPR can't be wrong.

Occasionally over the next few months I attempted to draw attention to related research, most pointedly in this post from March 4, 2006:

[...] Even in historic genres, it's possible to make a conscious effort to switch imaginative contexts. [...] Along those lines, I liked [*Kinds of Literature* by Alastair Fowler] more than I expected. Genre markers are (sometimes unintended) signals to a community. *Spotting* the markers isn't enough to tell us what they're doing there. Fowler seemed to get that.

A more recent good example is Richard A. McCabe's "Annotating Anonymity" in *Ma*°*king the Text* [ed. Joe Bray, Anne Henry, and Miriam Fraser]. Rather than just describing the archaisms and explanatory apparatus of The Shepheardes Calender as pastoral conventions, McCabe shows how they took advantage of (and sometimes had to work against) the specific model of Servius's Virgil commentaries.

I'm now finishing *Memory in Oral Traditions* by David C. Rubin. [...] Rubin explains certain generic conventions of epic, ballad, and counting-out rhymes as directly molded by the mechanisms of multi-generational verbal transmission, and backs it up with evidence.

On a more negative note, Franco Moretti's "Graphs" and "Trees" are strictly parasitic on texts which he keeps strictly at arm's length. Not what I'd call a healthy relationship. More successful interdisciplinary materialist approaches go beyond the confines of the English department. And although the nora project [see Matt Kirschenbaum's contribution] limits itself to textual analysis, it's with the reasonable aim of noticing textual aspects missed by received opinion.

Books don't compete with each other in a closed bibliosphere. Popularity and genre are *social*, not strictly *textual*. They can only be understood by looking outside a text itself. And when you do so, I think you find something more like chaos theory than like biological evolution.

Eventually, though, I think I got the message. *Graphs, Maps, Trees* wasn't a collection of research papers. It was a celebration, a manifesto whose solipsism gave it the appeal of a human interest story. Any questioning of its *results* would inevitably be taken as dissent from its *cause*. In more ways than one, my lack of enthusiasm was genre-based.

originally posted, January 11, 2006
http://www.thevalve.org/go/valve/article/i_graphs_maps_trees_by_franco_
moretti/

## Works Cited

Bourdieu, Pierre. "The Invention of the Artist's Life." *Yale French Studies* 73 (1987): 75-103.

Friedlander, Benjamin. *Simulcast: Four Experiments in Criticism*. 1st ed. U of Alabama Press, 2004.

Hart, Clive, and David Hayman. *James Joyce's Ulysses: Critical Essays*. U of California Press, 1977.

Perkins, David. *The Arts and Cognition*. Johns Hopkins University Press, 1977.

## Notes

1   "Some time in my teenage years I lost the ability to perceive the outside world as I had been doing, as if some kind of filter or screen had been brought between my senses and reality ..." http://www.bhikku.net/archives/02/mar02.html

2   "How does the artist convey the very epitome of feminine sensuality? What he does is simply take the average female form, subtract the average male form—you're going to get big breasts, big hips and a narrow waist. And then amplify it, amplify the difference. And you don't say: 'My God, it's anatomically incorrect'. You say: 'Wow! What a sexy goddess!'" From "Lecture 3: The Artful Brain," Reith Lectures 2003. http://www.bbc.co.uk/radio4/reith2003/lecture3.shtml

# ③ Poetry, Patterns, and Provocation: The nora Project

**MATTHEW KIRSCHENBAUM**

*[editor's note – Kirschenbaum's piece describes the nora project which has, subsequently, become part of the MONK project. Kirschenbaum's piece is especially interesting for its methodological reflections. Links have been updated.]*

What follows is a brief introduction to NORA [now MONK], an ongoing and experimental project in literature and computation. My thanks to The Valve for the opportunity to make our work part of the conversation here. While not directly inspired by Moretti's writing in *Graphs, Maps, Trees*, nora exhibits many of the same priorities: an emphasis on quantitative method, large-scale data analysis, visualization, abstract modeling, cooperation and collaboration. These are methods foreign to many in the humanities, as are our actual technologies which run the gamut from XML and Java to a toolkit developed by the Automated Learning Group at the National Center for Supercomputing Applications. Yet nora (which, depending on who you ask on the project team, originated as either an acronym for no one remembers acronyms or a character in the William Gibson novel *Pattern Recognition*—though we've since located other noras) is also about provocation, ambiguity, and ultimately, interpretation—in short, still the stuff most of us would identify as central to academic literary studies.

First, here's the official version of what we're doing:

The goal of the nora project is to produce software for discovering, visualizing, and exploring significant patterns across large collections of full-text humanities resources in existing digital libraries. In search-and-retrieval, we bring specific queries to collections of text and get back (more or less useful) answers to those queries; by contrast, the goal of data-mining (including text-mining) is to produce new knowledge by exposing unanticipated similarities or differences, clustering or dispersal, co-occurrence and trends. Over the last decade, many millions of dollars have been invested in creating digital library collections: at this point, terabytes of full-text humanities resources are publicly available on the web. Those collections, dispersed across many different institutions, are large enough and rich enough to provide an excellent opportunity for text-mining, and we believe that web-based text-mining tools will make those collections significantly more useful, more informative, and more rewarding for research and teaching. nora is currently in the second year of two years of funding from the Andrew W. Mellon Foundation. The Principal Investigator is John Unsworth, formerly director of the Institute for Advanced Technology in the Humanities at the University of Virginia, now Dean of the Graduate School of Library and Information Science at the University of Illinois, Urbana Champaign. Participating researchers are also based at the Universities of Georgia, Maryland, Virginia, and Alberta.

Now for the unofficial version:

All of this is very, very hard. For starters, none of the technical architecture for what we wanted to do was in place when we started. We were able to leverage several existing platforms and technologies but other pieces had to be built from scratch. At present, nora is held together with chewing gum and duct tape, a loose tissue of resources and standards (datastores, text mining engine, visualization toolkit and end-user interface) coupled with the more-than-occasional late night email or IM session when something isn't working. A significant part of our efforts to date have been devoted to stabilizing this architecture, and we're most of the way there at this point.

But we've also been spending our time trying to figure out what technologies like text mining are good for in humanities research, particularly literary studies. Were we in a social sciences discipline that routinely contends with large amounts of data or even perhaps a humanities discipline like history we would not have to work quite so hard. Literary scholars, however—here the force of Moretti's arguments make themselves felt—traditionally do not contend with very large amounts of data in their research. A significant component of our work is therefore basic research in the most literal sense: what kinds of questions do we seek to answer in literary studies and how can data mining help, or—more interestingly—what new kinds of questions can data mining provoke? (As a sidebar, we tried to answer that first one inductively. We compiled a list of verbs occurring in critical essays on 18th- and 19th-century British and American literature from journals in Project Muse that never or rarely occur in the American National Corpus, which is newspaper writing for the most part. In short, a portrait of a profession.) But the barriers to entry are non-trivial. To engage in data mining on its own turf demands fluency in terms like naïve Bayesian analysis, cosine similarity matrices, features, vectors, dendograms, decision trees, and neural networks. On the one hand we don't want to black box this stuff. We also don't want to build a system so intimidating that one needs an advanced degree in information science just to approach it.

Data mining and visualization are traditionally perceived as problem solving technologies. The canonical instance is Don Swanson's early use of text mining in bio-medical literature to identify a possible link between magnesium deficiency and migraine headaches. Swanson founds patterns of association in widely disparate areas of the published literature to make the initial connection, subsequently confirmed through a great deal of more traditional medical testing. He called his findings "undiscovered public knowledge"—it was all there, already in the journals, but no one had put the pieces together because no human reader would likely ever have been in a position to synthesize all of the relevant articles. But we don't typically set out to "solve" problems in the humanities. We're not trying to find the causes of migraines. We're not trying to "solve" the problem of Emily Dickinson so that we can move on to the even more urgent problem of Walt Whitman. So what does data mining have to offer literary interpretation?

To start, we're interested in provocation, anomaly, and outlier results as much or more than in what we think the system actually gets right. In one early proof of concept for nora, Steve Ramsay and Bei Yu attempted to classify Shakespeare's plays according to the traditional categories. The data mining got most of them right. That's not what was interesting though, at least not to Steve. What was interesting was that the data mining thought *Othello* might be a comedy. Interesting not because we're assigning any undue authority to the machine's determinations, but because the question became what was it about *Othello* that made it different from the other tragedies? Why did this dumb brute force machine "read" it as a comedy? As it happens, Steve subsequently stumbled across a strain of scholarship on the play that makes exactly that argument.

This initial experiment lead us down a path that produced the following kinds of questions, as recently articulated by John Unsworth: What patterns would be of interest to literary scholars? Can we distinguish between patterns that are, for example, characteristic of the English language, and those that are characteristic of a particular author, work, topic, or time? Can we extract patterns that are based in things like plot, or syntax? Or can we just find patterns of words? When is a correlation meaningful, and when is it coincidental? What does it mean to be "coincidental"? How do we train software to focus on the features that are of interest to researchers, and can that training interface be usable for people who don't like numbers and do like to read? Can we structure an interface that is sufficiently generalized that it can accommodate interest in many different kinds of features, without knowing in advance what they will be? What are meaningful visualizations, and how do we allow them to instruct their users on their use, while provoking an appropriate suspicion of what they appear to convey? How would we evaluate the effectiveness of our visualizations, or the software in general? Is it succeeding if it surprises us with its results, or if it doesn't? How can we make visualizations function as interfaces, in an iterative process that allows the user to explore and tinker? And how in the hell can we do all this in real time on the web, when a modest subset of our collection, like the novels of a single author, contain millions of datapoints, all of which need to be sifted for these patterns?

Our team at Maryland includes my colleague Martha Nell Smith in the English department, a long-time Emily Dickinson scholar. In order to focus our efforts I urged Martha and the rest of the team here to focus on the question of erotic language in Dickinson, certainly a well-turned question in the scholarship. We began with a corpus of about 200 XML-encoded letters comprising correspondence between the poet Emily Dickinson and Susan Huntington (Gilbert) Dickinson, her sister-in-law (married to her brother William Austin). The demo we produced requires a user to first rank an initial set of documents with which to train the automatic classifier. This is done on a scale of 1 to 5, a process we call hot or not for short. The process is not unlike the NetFlix interface that asks you to evaluate your favorite movies and then finds others that the recommender system thinks also might be to your liking. This initial training set is then delivered to the data mining engine, which proceeds to iterate over the rest of the document set and return its initial predictions. Users can see which individual words the data mining seized upon as potential indicators of the erotic. The method here, by the way, is known as *naïve bayes*. Bayesian probability is the domain of probability that deals with non-quantifiable events: not whether a coin will land heads or tails for instance, but rather the percentage of people who believe the coin might land on its side; also known as subjective probability. Our Bayesian classification is "naïve" because it deliberately does not consider relationships and dependencies between words we might instinctively think go together—"kiss" and "lips," for example. The algorithm merely establishes the presence or absence of one or more words, and takes their presence or absence into account when assigning a probability value to the overall text. ("Yeah, naïve, you, got that part right," I hear some of you saying. But this is the kind of thing computers are very good at, and naïve Bayes has been proven surprisingly reliable in a number of different text classification domains.) Right now the demo is hard-coded to the Dickinson corpus, but it will be general before we are through with nora.

As I hope should be clear, by far the least interesting aspect of this (to us) would be the machine's definitive conclusion as to whether Emily is hot or not (we think the answer to that is rather obvious). No, we're interested in the data mining's capacity for provocation. Here, for example, is Smith on some early results, when the word "mine" ranked high on the list of words the data mining thought might be hot:

The minute I saw it, I had one of those "I knew that" moments. Besides possessiveness, "mine" connotes delving deep, plumbing, penetrating—all things we associate with the erotic at one point or another. And Emily Dickinson was, by her own accounting and metaphor, a diver who relished going for the pearls. So "mine" should have been identified as a "likely hot" word, but has not been, oddly enough, in the extensive literature on Dickinson's desires. Same goes for "write"—oh to leave a piece of oneself with, for, the beloved. To "write" is to present oneself, or a piece of oneself, physically—and noting that the data mining was picking up both "write" when recorded by Dickinson and "write" in the [XML] header [where it would indicate a letter] led the three of us to a "can we teach a computer to recognize tone" discussion. I wonder, remembering Dickinson's "A pen has so many inflections and a voice but one" what the human machine can do, what the human machine does (recognizing, identifying tone) what we think we're doing when we're so damned sure of ourselves. So the data mining has made me plumb much more deeply into little four- and five-letter words, the function of which I thought I was already sure, and has also enabled me to expand and deepen some critical connections I've been making for the last 20 years.

We're currently in the midst of a second, larger experiment on reading sentimental novels from the Early American Fiction Collection at the University of Virginia. The steps we're following run something like this: **Stage 1**. Evaluate the use of text-mining on a small set of "core" sentimental novels. We will label a subset of the chapters (the training set) with a score indicating a level of sentimentalism, and then see how text mining classifies the remaining chapters from those novels. (Texts: *Charlotte, Uncle Tom's Cabin, Incidents in the*

*Life of a Slave Girl.*) **Stage 2**. Two more novels will be added to the set to evaluate how well the processes work when more texts by the same authors are added to the set of works studied. (Texts added: *Charlotte's Daughter, The Minister's Wooing.*) **Stage 3**. The texts added will be those that scholars recognize as exhibiting sentimentalism, though some may not be as consistently sentimental chapter-by-chapter as the "core" set used earlier. In this experiment there will be more focus on gaining insights on sentimentalism and these novels than in previous experiments. (Some likely texts: *Clotelle, The Lamplighter, The Coquette, Hobomok.*) **Stage 4**. Using a text-mining model that was developed to identify chapters with strong sentimentalism, use text-mining on a set of works that are considered by scholars not to be wholly sentimental or just not sentimental at all. This may identify parts of texts that contain aspects of sentimentalism, or common word-use that is sentimental in one novel but not another. In this experiment there will be a strong focus will be on gaining insights on sentimentalism and these novels. Texts: *Moby-Dick, The Scarlet Letter, The Blithedale Romance*, Irving's *Sketchbook, Narrative of the Life of Frederick Douglass.*)

There's more to say, including what students might get out of a process like this. Maybe I can address some of that in the comments. But just one more point here: Louis Menand, in the current issue of *Profession*, decries what he calls the "Captain Kangaroo" model of interdisciplinarity that pervades the humanities: putting a psychologist on the podium with a Freudian literary critic for a conference session, for example. When the full nora project team meets, we have literary scholars, computer scientists, and information specialists around the table. I have a Ph.D. in English, but at Maryland, in addition to Martha Nell Smith and Tanya Clement in the English department I work with Catherine Plaisant and James Rose in the Human Computer

Interaction Lab and Greg Lord at the Maryland Institute for Technology in the Humanities (MITH). Steve Ramsay at the University of Georgia is a gifted programmer as well as an Assistant Professor of English and his graduate student Sara Steger is both a serious scholar of the 19th century novel and a serious hacker. Similar teams exist at Virginia and Alberta. At Illinois, we're joined by personnel from the Graduate School of Library and Information Science (usually ranked as the finest library school in the country) and the National Center for Supercomputing Applications (NCSA). This collaboration is not always easy or idyllic. As Stanley Fish is said to have said somewhere, being interdisciplinary is hard. But the collaboration and mutual respect are real, and they are indispensable to getting things done. No one person has all of the expertise and knowledge at hand that a project like nora demands. I dare say that the graduate students working with us on the project, both from English and computer/information science, are exposed to a very different model of scholarly production, and different work habits, from what would typically be the case in their disciplines.

Okay, this really is the last thing I want to say: none of us see this as a messianic enterprise. We're not out to "save" the humanities. Graphs, maps, and trees may not be for everyone, nor is data mining I'm sure. But by the same token, none of what I have been describing here is extracurricular research for me or any of the other humanities scholars on the project team. It counts toward the research portion of my annual distribution of effort for one thing, and the publications and results go onto my vita. Moreover, I'm a member of the MLA (dues all paid up) and work from nora has already been presented there, to interested and receptive audiences. Let's all be a little careful with the generalizations and assumptions that have been flying around some of the previous entries. Cheers again to The Valve for getting this book event together.

originally posted, January 12, 2006
http://www.thevalve.org/go/valve/article/poetry_patterns_and_provocation_the_
nora_project/

## Works Cited

Menand, Louis. "Dangers, Within and Without." *Profession* (2005).

# ④ Book Notes: Franco Moretti's Graphs, Maps, and Trees

## Timothy Burke

Of all the odd things I've heard in recent years, one of the oddest would be that there are objections in principle to the research paradigm that Franco Moretti describes in *Graphs, Maps, Trees*. It really doesn't matter what your interest in cultural or literary analysis is: what Moretti proposes is useful grist for your mill. There is no requirement to purchase the entire methodological inventory he makes available, or to throw overboard close reading or aesthetic appreciation or focus on a small and rarefied set of texts. Frankly, when academics propose that we only do what they're doing and stop doing everything else, I tend to ignore such propositions in the same way that I ignore commercial hyperbole while deciding what things I want to buy. I enjoy my iPod: I'm not required to think that it has changed my life or should lead me to chuck my stereo out the window. Whatever you think literary analysis and cultural history are, quantifying the subject of their domains is a very good thing. Indeed, it is a kind of knowledge long inferred and rarely acquired, and though its acquisition unsettles some assumptions made in the inferred known, it equally clarifies and strengthens many other claims—or least puts new and productive burdens on them.

Leave aside for the moment the particular kinds of modelings and configurations of his data that Moretti describes, and just stick with the numbers alone. Even in a single national literature, it used to be hard to make any clear statements about the total number of books published in a given year or across a long series of years, and of those books, what proportion were works commonly known, analyzed, or regarded as defining a "literature." Now Moretti is not really so unusual or isolated as he might appear in taking an interest in such quantification, as Matt Greenfield has noted. There are many subfields of cultural history and literary analysis that have taken an interest in similar quantification and mapping, in fact, the study of genres has long been shaped by an interest in cycles of publication of the kind Moretti describes.

The numbers alone, as Moretti observes, immediately falsify or complicate a series of conventional ways of understanding cultural or literary change over time. When we speak of a particular novel's influence, or about how literature changed in response to a particular work, we're making claims that ought to involve a total topography of published cultural work. Until recently, that would not have been the case. If it turns out that that the lineal descendants of a novel regarded as influential are no more than half a percent of all work published over a ten-year period, this puts pressure on what we mean by "influential." It is not that we are now forbidden to make the claim, but it constrains and specifies what we can potentially mean by such a claim. It's just that Moretti does helps us to realize that often, in making such claims, we've put too much trust in the representations and attributions of authors and readers, which are just as produced and fantastical as any publicly uttered memories, just as Goffmanesque in their performance as any other presentation of self. It is not that we are forbidden either to speak of that novel's quality or desirability, of what we (and past readers) might have found enticing, inspiring, productive, mysterious in such a work. Moretti doesn't quantify the production of meaning, and even if he wanted to, he could not.

Enough on the simple virtues of Moretti's project. Of course cultural historians and literary critics need numbers, all of us, and godspeed to the counting and graphing. I'd love to see someone do something similar with major historical archives: count all the documents, all of them, and graph for me their types and forms. Historians live in their archives, but we don't really know them half as well as we ought to. We accept the categories that the archive offers us, and read along the pathways laid down. In researching consumerism and material culture in colonial Zimbabwe, I had to read horizontally across an archive for a topic that the archive itself did not recognize as lying within its confines, and the sense I got of what the archive contained was complicated considerably, relative to what I'd been expecting. Quantification could only help that understanding further.

What could enhance Moretti's work further? What do I see as genuine problems and gaps in the models he offers?

First, a warning: that counting publications only scratches the surface of the totality of cultural production in any given post-Gutenberg moment. This is an issue that RAPHAEL SAMUEL wrote about for years with regard to historians and their archives: that what lands in archives, is recorded as documentary evidence, is just a small and sometimes highly unrepresentative selection of the totality of potential grist for the historian's mill in a given era. Moretti may be counting formal publication and finding that what is commonly taken to represent "national literature" is not typical or representative, but beyond that lies an even larger domain composed of the ephemeral, the unpreserved, the unrecorded. In the age of electronic communication, we should be especially sensitive to this problem. Even with the Web being archived, much of what has been written within it, and read avidly, is likely to be lost in the longer-term: asynchronous discussions, epistolary literatures passing through email, and so on.

There will come a point at which a project of quantifying cultural production in any given historical moment will only be able to gesture at a vast Oort cloud of unknown writings, performances, and texts, seeing the gravitational effects of some unseeable and lost Planet X tugging at the knowable and quantified. This especially strikes me as an Africanist: we now have some lovely examples of "MARKET LITERATURE" IN NIGERIA available in published form, but beyond those examples, I very much doubt we will ever be able to represent the numbers or varieties of such texts published. If we confine our understanding of what was typical or normal within a cultural form to what we can find in archives, in libraries, in catalogs, in records of publication, we'll ultimately have a deformed conception of the totality. Beyond everything counted there is always another mountain of the uncountable. Historians of slavery turned over every stone and record to COUNT THE TOTAL NUMBERS OF AFRICANS taken across the Atlantic, and even then, had to make some educated guesses, which still fuels (sometimes quite intense) debate among specialists in that field. But once some numbers were in hand, those historians realized that making any statements about their meaning depended on another set of numbers, namely, how many people there were in West and Equatorial Africa at any given moment in any given society, what the fertility rates were in those places, the numbers of men and women, and so on. All numbers which, frankly, are never going to be tallied through anything besides serious guesswork.

The second thing that occurs to me on reading Moretti is that we know quantifying publication and quantifying discrete elements (tropes, places, and so on) within publications doesn't tell us half so much as we might think about the quantification of readership and circulation. Again, maybe it's because I'm an Africanist that I'm especially wary in this regard. You can count up the numbers of newspapers published in a decade in southern Africa, including ones presumptively aimed at African audiences. You would be making a big mistake to assume that such numbers tell you how many people were reading or consuming those newspapers. We know from historical and ethnographic work that the literate often read or reinterpreted newspapers for the illiterate, and that a single copy of a publication was often passed around many readers. Texts travel through readerships in ways that numbers do not describe very well. Here I'd look to Elizabeth Hofmeyr's fantastic book on the transnational history of John Bunyan's *Pilgrim's Progress* for some insight, for a tracing of how a single work can traverse readerships in ways not precisely correlated with its appearance in libraries, archives, or even within texts that invoke, allude or cite Bunyan. There ought to be a sociology and social history of audience and reading that might complement Moretti's work, but my intuitive suspicion is that it would also very much complicate the claims he would like to make. I also think that the sociology of authorship and publication would be a useful complement to Moretti: to know who knows whom, who reads whom, and to which outlets and forms of publication they relate strikes me as retaining its importance.

The most important concern I have about Moretti is that I think he has the same problem that the *Annalistes* and world-systems analysts have had with modernity: a difficulty explaining rupture, breach, or novelty. Novelty here in multiple senses: as Elif Batuman observes, the novel-form is what gets marked off in Moretti as something not explained. In world-systems history, this problem has lately been exaggerated to extremes by some of the founding practitioners in the field, as in Andre Gunder Frank's argument late in his life that the contemporary world-system is part of a continuous five-thousand year old history, that modernity or the rise of the West is a temporary or epiphenomenal speed bump in a well-worn road, not anything genuinely new. The problem with a divergent tree of literary or cultural history is that it has a hard time explaining the appearance of genuinely new forms or genres: it is forced always to insist on a fundamental continuity. The best that the world-systems historians could do, if they didn't want to follow Frank's argument that modernity or the rise of the West was an illusion, was either to insist on materialist explanations of rupture (new technologies, new means of production) or to offer shopworn dialectics.

In evolutionary terms, Moretti is something of a gradualist; my impulse is to throw up the cultural equivalent of punctuated equilibria in reply, to insist that some genres and forms do not descend gracefully from predicates but emerge abruptly, catastrophically, like Aphrodite stepping from the waves. The evolutionary metaphor is a powerful one, but you want to take in even more of it than Moretti does. For one, it's fine to talk about the death of forms and genres, about how divergence fuels convergence that fuels more divergence. You can't have a metaphor that invokes evolution or speciation without death, or at least the removal of specialized forms. But it begs the question (and Moretti knows that it does) of what the fitness landscape is for cultural forms.

'Emerge' in fact is the operative verb here: I think Moretti's trees in particular could benefit enormously from reference to the body of work subsumed under the heading of "emergence" or "complexity theory." Because there is an answer within that body of work to Moretti's question: what explains the divergence of literary forms? It's not an especially comforting answer, perhaps, for either Moretti or some of his critics, because it may eschew some deep underlying explanatory principle for why some genres, tropes, modes of literary representation produce an explosion of divergent forms and why others die. In an emergent system, the place within the topology of the system where complex structures appear may be effectively random. If we take Moretti's example of Sherlock Holmes, it might be that an evolutionary tree of British fiction in the last half of the 19th Century would help us to understand why the environment was friendly to "detective fiction," what the conditions of the cultural soil were like for the growing of a new tree. But as for how Doyle's stories set the conventions of a genre and others die, are forgotten or wither, some of that might be simply termed "dumb luck". The precise moment at which a genre crystallizes may involve accidents of readership, circulation, publication and imitation. We are not required to explain that moment by arguing that Doyle somehow uniquely intuited the needs and desires of a reading public, or was distinguished through extraordinary ability. I'm echoing Gould's *Wonderful Life* here very consciously. This is a rebuke of traditional literary theory, historicist literary theory and even Moretti all at once: all of them assume that there is a rational way to explain cultural reproduction which relates the successful, generative or meaningful text to some underlying condition of its being: an ideological or discursive fit to its environment, a skillful or superior authorial creation of an aesthetic, or some undiscovered underlying "law" of cycles and divergences. Here maybe Moretti needs to go the next step rather than running back for the materialist security blanket as he does in closing the book.

The accidental and the emergent are also, however, where we might reopen the door to agency, creativity and the will of the author and reader again. Because another thing that appears in literary and cultural history is the unpredictable generativity of authors and readers who reach from a high branch far back down the tree to create some new possibility of representation, who take what was a junk gene in DNA of culture and from it express some meaning or representation that was deemed impossible the day before. Sometimes such authors are just Carlo Ginzberg's Menocchio, envisioning private cultural worlds that die or are forgotten; sometimes they are better situated, differently located, or even, dare we say it, more imaginative or skillful in how they excavate the literary past in order to produce new possibility. Just as I would in the end say that modernity is an emergent and in some ways accidental social structure which in turn creates the possibility for individual agency that then generates still other emergent forms through will, choice or deliberate selection, I think you can reconcile the agency of authors and readers with Moretti's graphs, maps and trees, but it does take coloring outside his lines to do so.

originally posted, January 13, 2006

http://www.thevalve.org/go/valve/article/book_notes_franco_morettis_graphs_
maps_trees/

## Works Cited

Hofmeyr, Isabel. *The Portable Bunyan: A Transnational History of "The Pilgrim's Progress."* Princeton University Press (2003).

# ⑤ A Brief Note on Moretti and Science Fiction

**ADAM ROBERTS**

Towards the end of "Graphs," Moretti touches briefly on SF: neither Detective Fiction nor SF, he says, are included on his chart, "although both genres achieve their modern form about 1890 (Doyle, Wells) and undergo a major change in the 1920s, in step with the overall pattern." Nevertheless, he concedes, "their long duration seems to require a different approach."

Well, I've just published the result of several years work designed to argue the case that SF has enjoyed a longer duration even than Moretti is inclined to allow. Not that he takes an unusual position with regard to the genre. There are, in a nutshell, three main views as to when SF "began": it began with Mary Shelley's *Frankenstein* in 1818; it began with H. G. Wells's *Time Machine* in 1895; it began with Hugo Gernsback's magazine *Amazing Stories* in 1926, and Gernsback's prosodically-hobbledehoy coinage "scientifiction." Moretti is arguing, broadly, that novel genres have about a quarter-century lifespan, which, even if we chose the latest possible starting place as a launching point, does indeed give SF a "long duration."

In my book, however, I try to make the case for the "long history" of SF. I argue that science fiction began at the beginning of the seventeenth-century, with Kepler's *Somnium* (written c.1600, published 1634). My argument is more complicated than this. But for now I want to outline one way in which my 400-year version of SF chimes with Moretti's very persuasive claims for a "generational" structure to the development of novelistic forms. I proceed without teams of researchers, graphs, or indeed anything other than the brain-cram of only recently having finished writing my Palgrave book—which is to say, I proceed tentatively. But if Moretti is right then perhaps we need to be looking at SF not so much as a "novelistic genre" and more as a cultural mode; for we find within it certain approximately generational "vogues," which might be sketched as follows:

1. **1600s-1650s**: Lunar adventure. Kepler's *Somnium* 1600-36; John Wilkins, *The Discovery of a World in the Moone* (1638); William Godwin *The Man in the Moone* (1638); Cyrano de Bergerac, *L'Autre Monde ou les Etats et Empires de la lune* [*Voyage dans la Lune*] (1657).

2. **1650s-1690s**: Philosophical speculation and "the plurality of worlds." Athanasius Kircher, *Iter exstaticum coeleste* (1656); Bernard de Fontenelle, *Entretiens sur la pluralité des mondes* (1686); Gabriel Daniel, *Voyage du Monde de Descartes* (1690).

3. **1700s-1750s**: The alien as fantastical humanoid (encountered on earth, within earth or near above earth). Jonathan Swift, *Gulliver's Travels* (1726); Voltaire's *Micromégas* (1750); Thomas Gray, "Luna habitabilis" (1737); Ludvig Holberg, *Nikolai Klimi iter subterraneum* (1741); Robert Paltock, *The Life and Adventures of Peter Wilkins* (1750).

4. **1750s-1790s**: The fantastic voyage as satiric-comic buffoonery (often with pointed political allegory); this is of course something already noticeable in Swift

and Voltaire, but made much coarser, ruder and more obvious in: "Sir Humphrey Lunatic," *A Trip to the Moon: Containing an Account of the Island of Noibla* (1764); Tobias Smollett, *The History and Adventures of an Atom* (1769), William Thomson's *The Man in the Moon; or, Travels into the Lunar Regions by the Man of the People* (1783) and the two anonymous works *A Journey Lately Performed Through the Air in an Aerostatic Globe* (1784) and *A Voyage to the Moon, Strongly Recommended to All Lovers of Real Freedom* (1793).

**5. 1760s-1800s**: Utopian, and future fictions. These two things, perhaps unsurprisingly, go together with and reinforce the climate that produced the French Revolution and its aftermath: the anonymous *The Reign of George VI: 1900-1925* (1763); Louis Sebastien Mercier, *L'An 2440* (1771); Nicolas-Edme Restif de la Bretonne, *La découverte australe par un homme volant* (1781); John Wessel *Anno 7603* (1781); Restif, *Les Posthumes* (1805).

**6. 1810s-1850s:** Monsters, Mummies, Automata: Gothic Heritage SF [Hoffman, *Der Sandmann* (1816); Mary Shelley, *Frankenstein* (1818); Jane Loudon, *The Mummy! A Tale of the Twenty-Second Century* (1827)].

**7. 1800s-1850s.** Tales of the far future/last man tales. Cousin de Grainville *Le dernier homme* (1805); Mary Shelley, *The Last Man* (1826); Felix Bodin, *Le Roman de l'avenir* (1834); Prince Vladimir Odoevsky, "4338 i-god" ("The year 4338," 1840); R. F. Williams, *Eureka: a Prophesy of the Future* (1837); Tennyson "Locksley Hall" (1841); Anon, *The Air Battle. A Vision of the Future* (1859).

**8. 1860s-1890s**: Travel through the solar system by Anti-Gravity devices. The first novel to use this device is Joseph Atterley, *A Voyage to the Moon* (1827), but it doesn't really get going until later in the century with: "Chrysostom Trueman," *The History of a Voyage to the Moon* (1864); Percy Greg, *Across the Zodiac: the Story of a Wrecked Record* (1880); John Jacob Astor, *A Journey to Other Worlds* (1894); Frank Stockton, "A Tale of Negative Gravity" (1884); H. G. Wells" *The First Men in the Moon* (1901).

**9. 1870-1900s**: Near-future Invasion fictions. Chesney, *The Battle of Dorking* (1871); Horace Lester's *The Taking of Dover* (1888); Louis Tracy, *The Final War* (1896); Erskine Childers, *The Riddle of the Sands* (1903); William Le Quex, *The Invasion of 1910: With a Full Account of the Siege of London* (1906).

**10. 1880s-1910s**: Utopias. Edward Bellamy, *Looking Backward 2000-1887* (1888); William Morris, *News From Nowhere, or An Epoch of Rest* (1890); H. G. Wells, *A Modern Utopia* (1905); Charlotte Perkins Gilman, *Herland* (1915).

**11. 1890s-1920s**: Interplanetary conflict. Kurd Lasswitz, *Auf Zwei Planeten* (1897); H. G. Wells, *The War of the Worlds* (1898); Edgar Rice Burroughs, *Under the Moons of Mars* (published in book form as *A Princess of Mars*, 1912).

**12. 1910s-1930s**: Gernsbackian SF: first phase of Pulp SF. Hugo Gernsback, *Ralph 124C 41+* (1911-12); E. E. Doc Smith, *The Skylark of Space* (1928);

*Triplanetary* (1934); Jack Williamson, *The Legion of Space* (1934).

**13. 1920s-1930s:** Spectacle and Monsters: first phase of SF cinema. Rene Clair, *Paris qui dort* (1923); Fritz Lang, *Metropolis* (1926); James Whale, *Frankenstein* (1931); Merian C. Cooper and Ernest B. Schoedsack, *King Kong* (1933); William Cameron Menzies, *Things to Come* (1936).

**14. 1920s-1940s.** Machinic Dystopia. Yevgeny Zamiatin, *We* (1920); Fritz Lang's *Metropolis* (1927); Aldous Huxley's *Brave New World* (1932); Rene Barjavel, *Ravage* (1943); Hermann Kasack, *Die Stadt hinter dem Strom* (1946), George Orwell's *Nineteen-Eighty Four* (1949).

**15. 1930s-1950s:** Campbellian or "Golden Age" SF. John W. Campbell becomes editor of *Astounding* (1938); Robert Heinlein, "The Roads Must Roll" (1940); Isaac Asimov "Nightfall" (1941); A. E. Van Vogt, *Slan* (1946); Robert Heinlein *Starship Troopers* (1959).

**16. Late 1930-1960s:** Superhero Comics. *Superman* (from 1938); "Captain Marvel," (Whiz Comics from 1940); *Batman* (from 1940); "Captain America" (from 1941); John Broome and Gil Kane's reinvention of "The Green Lantern" (from 1959); *The Fantastic Four* (from 1961); *Spider-Man* (from 1962); *X-Men* (from 1963); *The Silver Surfer* (from 1968).

**17. 1950s-1960s:** Classic SF Cinema Irving Pichel, *Destination Moon* (1950); Inoshiro Honda, *Gojira* (1954); Fred McLeod Wilcox, *Forbidden Planet*

(1956); Don Siegel, *Invasion of the Body Snatchers* (1956); George Pal, *The Time Machine* (1960).

**18. 1950s-1960s**: Cosy-catastrophes. John Wyndham, *Day of the Triffids* (1950); Arthur C. Clarke, *Childhood's End* (1953); John Wyndham, *The Midwich Cuckoos* (1957); John Christopher, *The World in Winter* (1962).

**19. Late 1950s-1980s**: Messianic and Religious SF. James Blish, *A Case of Conscience* (1958); Walter Miller, *A Canticle for Leibowitz* (1959); Robert Heinlein, *Stranger in a Strange Land* (1961); Frank Herbert, *Dune* (1965); Roger Zelazny, *Lord of Light* (1967); Michael Moorcock, *Behold the Man* (1969); Sheri Tepper, *Grass* (1989); Dan Simmons, *Hyperion* (1989), Gene Wolfe, *Book of the Long Sun* (1993-96).

**20. 1960s**. Psychedelic or Hallucinatory SF. Philip K Dick, *The Three Stigmata of Palmer Eldritch* (1965); Michael Moorcock, *The Final Programme* (1969); Stanley Kubrick, *2001: A Space Odyssey* (1968); Philip K. Dick, *Ubik* (1969); David Bowie, "Space Oddity" (1969).

**21. 1960s-1980s**. Gender SF. Ursula Le Guin, *The Left Hand of Darkness* (1969); Joanna Russ, *The Female Man* (1975); Margaret Atwood, *The Handmaid's Tale* (1985); Sheri Tepper, *The Gate to Women's Country* (1988).

**22. 1977-2000s**. Blockbuster SF Cinema. George Lucas, *Star Wars* (1977); Steven Spielberg, *Close Encounters of the Third Kind* (1977); Ridley Scott, *Alien* (1979); Spielberg, *E.T.* (1982); James Cameron,

*Terminator* (1984); Spielberg, *War of the Worlds* (2005).

**23. 1980-2000s**. Cyberpunk. Ridley Scott, *Blade Runner* (1982); William Gibson, *Neuromancer* (1984), Masamune Shirow, *Kokaku Kidotai* ("Ghost in the Shell" 1991), Neal Stephenson, *Snow Crash* (1994), Wachowski brothers, *Matrix* trilogy (1999-2003).

A couple of notes on this. Firstly, of course there's a lot of wiggle-room in these little categories. They've been arrived at subjectively and are meant to identify the core vogues for their respective topics rather than the exhaustive categorization of the field. (So for instance, obviously, plenty of utopias were written after 1915; although I'd still argue that the immediate wake of Bellamy's book saw the real heart of the vogue). Secondly, I'm aware that were I to plot these out on a graph they'd look a lot like the graph in "Graphs" ... Figure 9, to be specific. Make of that what you will.

originally posted, January 13, 2006

http://www.thevalve.org/go/valve/article/a_brief_note_on_moretti_and_science_
fiction/

## Works Cited

Roberts, Adam. *The History of Science Fiction*. Palgrave, 2006.

# ⑥ Maps, Iconic and Abstract

## WILLIAM BENZON

Though I am rather interested in maps, I admit to being a bit puzzled by the maps chapter of Moretti's book. Part of my problem is that I am comfortable, not only with the iconic maps of physical space that Moretti uses, but with the notion of a cognitive map as used by psychologists and neuroscientists, and with abstract maps of conceptual spaces used by cognitive and computer scientists. I have given considerable thought to the use of those abstract maps of conceptual spaces in the study of (literary) textual semantics. Moretti is not doing that sort of thing in this chapter, which is fine. My problem is that I don't quite see how to relate what he has done with iconic maps to thinking that I—and others—have done in terms of abstract conceptual maps.

I say this, not as a criticism of his chapter, but as a statement of my difficulty in engaging with that chapter. This document is a set of comments around and about that, but arriving at no particular conclusion. It is an essay into possible sites of exploration.

## Cognitive Maps

Let me start with the cognitive map, which is a neuro-cognitive structure through which an animal "represents" the external world. The nature of this representation is of considerable interest to psychologists and has attracted a good deal of attention. This work is closely related to the mechanisms by which animals navigate from one place to another. I have, at one time or another, read some of this literature, but I am not expert in it. The following remarks are meant to be no more than reasonable and indicative.

Animals are creatures of habit. They live in relatively fixed territories where various places serve various needs. There is a privileged place that serves as home base and there are various other places where the animal finds food and water, or danger. Many animals migrate with the seasons, sometimes over considerable distances. Finally, we should note that most animals are considerably more sensitive to odors than we are. They smell their way about the world. How is all this represented in the animal's brain?

There is no reason to believe that cognitive maps are like iconic maps except, rather than being inscribed in the dirt, or on a rock, or imprinted on paper, they are somehow inscribed in neural tissue. They seem to be more like lists of significant places intertwined with bearings and headings between one place and another. The *vital significance* of these places is *part and parcel* of the map; the "map" is not a neutral spatial substrate to which vital significance is later attached. The space of cognitive maps is not merely about physical position; it is about needs and satisfiers, vantage points and opportunities for action.

Given the importance of local and distant geography to animals, it is clear that the neural systems that map that geography must be sophisticated and complex (and have evolved over hundreds of millions of years). Other than the system for interpersonal relationships, these may be the most sophisticated neural systems we have. The myth narratives Levi-Strauss has analyzed in, e.g. *The Raw and the Cooked*, would appear to intertwine these two neuro-cognitive systems, the geographical and the social.

Vital significance seems central to Moretti's maps. It is not just that things happen in different places, but that different kinds of things happen at different kinds of places. And where people tell stories about the world around them, those stories will reflect the vital structure of that world.

One wonders how conscious were the writers of the geographic structure of their world. Some years ago Donald Norman asked graduate students living in a certain building—some of them for years—to sketch a map of their apartment (Norman, 139). Many of them made a significant error in their sketch, even thought they were sitting in the apartment when they made the sketch. Yet, they had no trouble getting around in the apartment building. Their mental model was adequate to that task, but not to the task of making a sketch. Would the authors of Moretti's texts have been able to make accurate sketches of the territory they wrote about? We do not know. But being able to make such sketches is quite a different skill from being able to navigate through the territory. In drawing his maps Moretti may thus show us something about the geography of those worlds that the writers themselves did not (quite) know.

They need not have been conscious of the lay of the land—as it appears to map makers—in order for it to be implicit in their narratives. If activities are arrayed in the world in a certain spatial pattern, and the narratives faithfully represent those activities, then that pattern will be implicit in the narrative without the author ever having given explicit thought to the structure of that array. If the usage of geography changes over time, then stories told over the same time span will reflect those changes. Again, without the author's being explicitly aware of this.

This is at the center of Moretti's arguments in the maps chapter. And perhaps that is what so interests him, that the narratives accurately reflect things of which the authors were not, need not have been, explicitly aware. Those patterns turn up in the narrative because that is how the world works. The world creeps into the mind in ways that exceed our explicit grasp.

### Ring Structures

Because our lives are lived in geography, many of our narratives include journeys within them or take the form of a journey. Some of those narratives even include maps as part of the text—I'm thinking of e.g. *Treasure Island*, *King Solomon's Mines*, or, rather more recently, *Perdido Street Station*. And then we have those squiggles in *Tristram Shandy* which map, not the places of Tristram's or Toby's or Walter's life, but the digressive mode of the telling.

Those squiggles are more abstract in their import. This leads me, in Shandian fashion, to ring structures, which are about the mode of telling. In the small, we have a rhetorical figure called chiasmus. For example, "well knows ... knows well" in Shakespeare's Sonnet 129: "This the world well knows, that none knows well . . . . " But such inversions appear in longer texts. (And they are an explicit part of the arsenal of melodic variation and development in baroque counterpoint.) A narrative will unfold through a series of steps to a mid-point and then trace its way back through the same series of steps, but in reverse, thus:

1 2 3 ... X ... 3' 2' 1'

Mary Douglas has been investigating ring structure in books of the Old Testament, while I have found it in Osamu Tezuka's graphic novel, *Metropolis*. The fact that rings are symmetrical about a mid-point suggests to me that they may ultimately depend on the cognitive structures we use for use for spatial navigation. If you travel from location A to N and then back you will pass the same landmarks on each half of the journey, but in reverse order. If things of interest and consequence happen to you along the way, both going and coming, then you may have a narrative that is interesting as well.

But the ring structure of Tezuka's narrative cannot be explained through fidelity to an external geography. For it is not physical movement in space that takes the form of a ring, nor the deployment of locations in space. Tezuka's narrative is more like a picture within a frame3 within a frame2 within a frame1, where you start at the outermost frame, move to the next, the next, then the picture, and then you turn around and go back out through the series of frames. We can think of frame1 as the public world at large; frame2 is an underground world of evil conspirators and robot slaves; while frame3 is a children's world, of home, schoolhouse, and playground. (The picture itself has starting revelations.) Beyond the fact that frame2 is underground, there is no explicit sense the geographic relationships between these realms nor even of different locations within each of the realms.

There is no particular reason to believe that Tezuka achieved this effect through conscious deliberation. The ring structure I've outlined is not at all obvious; uncovering it takes a bit of analytical work. Whatever forces are at work in this ring seem to me more mysterious than the material forces working on the English and German geography arrayed in the narratives Moretti examines. In those narratives the mind mirrors the external world. In Tezuka it is not clear that the mind is mirroring anything at all.

Note that these ring-form narrative are different from the rings Moretti talks about. In his discussion of village narratives he illustrates physical rings in the geography that is the setting for narratives. Certain things happen in the center, other things happen closer to the periphery. But nowhere does he talk about individual narratives having episodes arrayed in a cyclic fashion.

Thus the geographic ring and the narrative ring are different and independent phenomenon. Yet there is the possibility that the narrative ring ultimately depends on neural structures that arose for the purpose of navigating the physical world. The narrative ring is more abstract. Let us now consider a different kind of navigational abstraction.

### The Method of Loci

[Here I simply quote from an old article of mine on Visual Thinking (Benzon 1990)]:

> The *locus classicus* for any discussion of visual thinking is the method of loci, a technique for aiding memory invented by Greek rhetoricians and which, over a course of centuries, served as the starting point for a great deal of speculation and practical elaboration—an intellectual tradition which has been admirably examined by Frances Yates. The idea is simple. Choose some fairly elaborate building, a temple was usually suggested, and walk through it several times along a set path, memorizing what you see at various fixed points on the path. These points are the loci which are the key to the method. Once you have this path firmly in mind so that you can call it up at will, you are ready to use it as a memory aid. If, for example, you want to deliver a speech from memory, you conduct an imaginary walk through your temple. At the first locus you create a vivid image which is related to the first point in your speech and then you "store" that image at the locus. You repeat the process for each successive point in the speech until all of the points have been stored away in the loci on the path through the temple. Then, when you give your speech you simply start off on the imaginary path, retrieving your ideas from each locus in turn.

The technique could also be used for memorizing a speech word-for-word. In this case, instead of storing ideas at a loci, one stored individual words.

The method of loci has become a central part of our "memory improvement" lore. Further, the effectiveness of this technique has been verified in psychological laboratories. According to Ulric Neisser, a cognitive psychologist, it even works for people who deny that they have mental images.

What is interesting about this technique is that it involves the deliberate creation of a cognitive model that is affectively and motivationally neutral. One memorizes a particular physical space simply as a set of loci and paths between them. The loci have no intrinsic significance. Rather, they are mental "pigeon holes" in which one can place things that do have significance. What kind of "things"? Anything you can imagine.

Notice, in particular, how there is no necessary relationship between the topographic structure of the loci and the logical structure of whatever is committed to memory through those loci. If you were to listen to someone deliver a speech which he or she had committed to memory using the method of loci, there would be nothing in the speech that would betray the building used to establish the loci and the path used to traverse them. It would, in principle, be possible for two people to deliver pretty much the same speech, while using different buildings as their memory model.

That, in general, is the problem we face in trying to figure out how the mind deals with literary texts. However visible the texts, the mind's mechanisms are hidden. Moretti's maps tell us something of how the mind finds the world. But just how is it that the world makes its way into the mind there to be transformed into texts? That process remains invisible.

originally posted, January 14, 2006

http://www.thevalve.org/go/valve/article/maps_iconic_and_abstract/

## Works Cited

Benzon, William "Visual Thinking," A. Kent and J. G. Williams, Eds. *Encyclopedia of Computer Science and Technology*. Volume 23, supplement 8. Marcel Dekker, 1990, 411-427.

Norman, D. A. "Memory, Knowledge, and the Answering of Questions.) *Contemporary Issues in Cognitive Psychology: The Loyola Symposium*. R. L. Solso, ed. Wiley, 1973, 135-165.

# ⑦ a Hundred Flowers

## ERIC HAYOT

## Part I: Let a hundred flowers bloom

Moretti's work only becomes a "problem" for literary studies when it claims that its method ought to replace the ones currently in use. So far as I know it does not. Ergo: what's the problem? Let a hundred flowers bloom. The more ways we have of studying what we're interested in, the better.

There may be problems with the metaphors or with the statistics Moretti uses. Christopher Prendergast makes the case against certain of Moretti's moves fairly clear in his *NLR* response (the short version, focused on the argument in "Trees": there's no reason to suppose culture functions like nature). This is fine; the "rest" of literary studies is also a place filled with people arguing about the validity of one methodology or another. No one says that we should all stop using etymologies to close read because Heidegger knowingly used false ones. Let a hundred flowers bloom.

If it can be improved or modified—and of course it can—then Moretti's method (call it distant reading, Annales-style *longue durée* historicism, or sociology of literature) will benefit from having more people engaged in it. Presumably these people will disagree. This will increase the number of epistemological possibilities, some of which will prove more convincing than others. Perhaps even that movement could be the subject of a Moretti-style evolutionary study. In any case: let a hundred flowers bloom.

Why, then, is Moretti's work controversial? Partly because what he is doing is new and interesting, and partly because it comes at a moment when the last major wave of new ideas seems to have foundered. Many people seem to want a new Theory to replace the exhausted old Theory. These people need to relax. Moretti is like a guy who shows up to the party with liquor right after the keg has been emptied. Part of why he is welcome is because he is saving some people from boredom or despair (he writes: "it is precisely in the name of theoretical knowledge that 'Theory' should be forgotten, and replaced with the extraordinary array of conceptual constructions—theories, plural, and with a lower case 't'—developed by the natural and the social sciences" ("Trees," 63).) People who are desperate to cling to the old keg—either because they have grown to love it, or because they think there's still beer in there—sometimes feel threatened by the new guy at the party, and want to say that he shouldn't be at the party at all. But surely there's room for the beer drinkers and the liquor drinkers in the room; let a hundred flowers bloom. In this I am more catholic than Moretti himself, who in the lines I cite above seems to want everyone to move away from the keg and get to the good stuff they're drinking over at the science fraternities.

From another perspective what Moretti is doing is not that new at all. Louis Menand points out in a *Profession* 2005 essay that literary studies has always transformed itself by borrowing wholesale from other disciplinary structures. "Theory" as a branch (so thick it became a root) of literary studies produced its momentum out of encounters with linguistics (Saussure, Jakobson), anthropology (Lévi-Strauss), sociology (the Frankfurt School, Bourdieu), psychology (Freud, Lacan), history (Canguilhem, Foucault) and philosophy (Derrida, Levinas, Nancy, Lyotard, not to mention Marx, Hegel, and so on). The "real" linguists, anthropologists, sociologists and philosophers go on to decry literary studies' adulteration of their ideas; rinse and repeat. In this sense the newness of Moretti is just the kind of newness we in literary studies have always wanted. I would not be surprised if this newness operates on 25-year, generational cycles (though in the academic humanities you might have to account for the distortions produced by the nine years it takes, on average, to get a Ph.D).

Will I go on to do Moretti-style studies of literature? No; close reading mixed with deconstructive theory makes me happiest. Would I welcome someone doing Moretti's kind of work as a colleague? Of course I would. Will I suspect such a colleague of falling too far into sociology and forgetting about language? Will I wonder if s/he has turned the *longue durée* into a fetish? Certainly. But that's what argument and conversation are for; flowers don't just pollinate themselves.

### Part two: what's so funny 'bout peace, love, and interpretation?

The most polemical thing Moretti writes appears in the last paragraph of "Trees," where he says that his approaches "share a clear preference for explanation over interpretation." This reminds me of Lindsay Waters' recent piece in the *Chronicle* (already blogged about on The Valve by MIRIAM BURSTEIN and DANIEL GREEN). Waters claims that a recent book by Walter Benn Michaels exemplifies what's gone wrong with English in the past forty years: "the complete and total ascendancy of hermeneutics. Instead of the erotics of art, we've got the neurotics of art: the meaning-mongering of interpretation for its own sake."

What's wrong with interpretation? It sucks the life out of beauty, says Waters. It can't see "the larger structures within which [novels] have meaning in the first place," says Moretti. Both these claims seem ridiculous to me, Waters' because he has no idea what I think of as beautiful, and Moretti's because of the word "first."

But that's not really want I want to talk about: rather it seems interesting to me that two people who couldn't, presumably, disagree more about what literary studies should do and be (for Waters "beauty" is not in graphs or maps but in the ineffable experience of reading) both decide to frame their remarks as an attack on the primacy ("first" again) of interpretation. As Prendergast points out in his *NLR* piece, these claims are, of course, interpretations. Amateur deconstruction aside, however (not that Prendergast himself is either amateur or deconstructive), one might wonder—and this is a historical question sustained by a close reading—why right now, in January 2006, "interpretation" has become the word for what's wrong with literary studies (as Waters points out, Sontag's "Against Interpretation" is now 40 years old). A serious historical answer to this question would require recourse to the kind of resources marshaled by a Nora project or the gang at Google, or an army of graduate students, or perhaps just a few more hours of time than I'm willing to spend on it.

Nonetheless let me gesture towards an answer by suggesting that "interpretation" actually means something different in each case. For Waters (as for Sontag) "interpretation" valorizes the study of the text as a hermeneutic exercise blind to aesthetic pleasure. Making the text speak as an instance of pseudo-philosophy (this is what Keats is telling us about the relation between truth and beauty), pseudo-architecture (this is how Keats tells us about that relation), or pseudo-history (this is what Keats tells us about the understanding of truth and beauty in his era) instrumentalizes the beauty that is the subject of the text in the "first" place, and thus constitutes a kind of technologization of the real that is part of the life-destroying force of modernity (my rhetoric here matching Waters', if you care to read his piece).

For Moretti, on the other hand, "interpretation" suggests a kind of belletristic focus on the text at the expense of the "larger structures" and "temporal cycles" within which the form, as the subject of a materialist history, operates. Interpretation does not arrive at the "first" place of the text because it fetishizes local meaning at the expense of historical materialism. Though Moretti believes that no "single explanatory framework may account for the many levels of literary production and their multiple links with the larger social system," what he's interested in are "production" and "social systems," not interpretations which are themselves presumably only expressions of those systems or attempts to ignore them.

My theory of the historically negative force of "interpretation" in January 2006 will, it seems, have to account for the fact that "interpretation" means different things to different people who could nonetheless, through a distant enough reading, be seen to be arguing against the same thing. Does this "close" (not that close, frankly) reading of "interpretation" suggest that a more "distant" historical analysis of its appearance has lost all claim to the truth? No, because it still matters, I think, that the word "interpretation" is used in both cases. But I am suggesting that such a distant reading without an accompanying close reading will be missing out on at least some of the truth, just as a myopic focus on the difference between these uses of interpretation will fail to grasp the broader historical context within which they function. There is no room for "first" or "second" place in such a scheme. Rather there is an accommodating sense that no one method has all the answers, one that should produce a corresponding modesty about interpretive claims.

I say it again: let a hundred flowers bloom. This is not a simple metaphor (just ask the ones Mao beheaded). Blooming is connected to reproduction, which is, as Moretti knows, a competitive process. In a few generations some flowers will be gone, and new ones will emerge; there's not enough room in the field for everyone. Some very good people will be kept out by the dominant modes of criticism—try writing a dissertation on "hubris in Byron" these days and see how far it gets you—and some others will flower perhaps even more than they deserve, thanks to shifts in the critical winds. But the field of literary studies is not the same as a field in nature, the difference being that in literature the blooms exert some control (never as much as they'd like) over their environment. Letting others bloom requires opening yourself to the possibility of being taken, or overtaken, by the other flowers in the field, allowing yourself to be seduced by the idea that in the long run someone else is more important than you. That admission can cripple you, or it can return as an affirmation. Molly, blooming, knew this:

> "I was a Flower of the mountain yes when I put the rose in my hair like the Andalusian girls used or shall I wear a red yes and how he kissed me under the Moorish wall and I thought well as well him as another and then I asked him with my eyes to ask again yes and then he asked me would I yes to say yes my mountain flower and first I put my arms around him yes and drew him down to me so he could feel my breasts all perfume yes and his heart was going like mad and yes I said yes I will Yes"

originally posted, January 14, 2006
http://www.thevalve.org/go/valve/article/a_hundred_flowers/

## Works Cited

Menand, Louis. "Dangers, Within and Without." *Profession* (2005).

Waters, Lindsay. "Literary Aesthetics: the Very Idea." *The Chronicle of Higher Education* 16 Dec 2005. http://chronicle.com/weekly/v52/i17/17b00601.htm.

# ⑧ Moretti Responds

**FRANCO MORETTI**

Many thanks to everybody writing about the book—and four brief rejoinders.

Does work like mine belong in a History department, rather than in English? I take the idea as a compliment— trying to make literary study a part of historical research has always been a fixation of mine. Does this abolish the pleasure of reading literature? No—it just means that between the pleasure and the knowledge of literature [or at least a large part of knowledge] there is no continuity. Knowing is not reading.

Are literary cycles limited to the 19th century? I doubt it. Virtually all the evidence I know of [from studies in French, British, and other Western European literatures] points to the existence of genre cycles well before then, and the 20th century largely confirms the pattern, in literature and outside [think of war films, or westerns]. Of course, it remains to be seen how much of the literary [and cultural] field is affected by cycles. But even if it's only 50%, wouldn't that be a significant find?

Is it possible that relying on secondary sources may produce distortions? Of course. Point out a large enough number of distortions, and I will abandon the enterprise. But I'm not going to do so simply because of the "possibility" of a distortion. I firmly believe in falsifiability, but falsification is a matter of fact, not of possibility.

Do maps reveal very little about literature? Well, it depends. Those of village stories, for instance, bring to light a type of spatial perception that would be hard to envisage otherwise. The map of Paris from the *Atlas*—especially in connection with the London maps from the same book—explains why youth and social class play such different roles in the two traditions. And so on. Still, a lot of people have that reaction to maps—"Of course things are this way. What's the big deal?" So, may I suggest a little wager-experiment? Sometime in the future I'd like to make maps of regional narratives [Hardy, Verga]. Why don't map-skeptics write in advance what I will "obviously" find—and we compare the results once the maps are done?

originally posted, January 12, 2006
http://www.thevalve.org/go/valve/article/moretti_responds/

# ⑨ Moretti Responds (II)

**FRANCO MORETTI**

Some more thoughts:

First, a few details. I am less alone than I claim. Excellent. I didn't even know of the existence of the nora project, which seems very interesting, and I have now several new titles on my reading list, which is great. As for evolutionary approaches, I would be more cautious; some of them—like memetics, or the recent *Literary Animal* collection—strike me as naïve in their disregard for formal analysis, and passion for fuzzy or crude units of content.

Maps, no, there I am really alone, unfortunately (the idea of a literary atlas began as a collective project, and I ended up working on my own only when the first project was denied funding, and dissolved). Even Bill Benzon's very interesting post, as he says right away, is on a different type of map (his final question—how is it that the world makes its way into the mind there to be transformed into texts?—is however one of the truly Great Questions in front of us. I wish I knew what to answer).

One caveat for the more optimistic contributors. The field of, loosely speaking, science and literature is full of false starts. The best example of quantitative analysis ever done—Burrows' multivariate analysis of Austen's style—was published 20 years ago, and has had, if I'm not mistaken, hardly any effects. (No one has mentioned it in the course of this discussion either.) We're all working uphill, and I'm not sure it's going to change soon.

Close reading and abstract models, or, interpretation and explanation. Bill Benzon is absolutely right in saying that even in the sciences research is not evenly spread, but clusters around specific issues—the fruit fly is a particularly neat example, because detective fiction is a sort of literary fruit fly (with few and clear variables, easy to manipulate). But this is not close reading, it's actually much more similar to the "experiments" (on village stories etc.) that I try to do in the book. So, I still think that the strategies I outlined are antithetical to the mainstream of literary criticism. It may be tactically silly for me to say so now, given that the general consensus is that what I do could be interesting, as long as it doesn't want to get rid of current procedures, but what can I do, this is not a matter of bragging, or of originality (originality, in a book that borrows all its models?!), or of democracy (a hundred flowers, yes, and more)— it's a matter of logic. Between interpretation (that tends to make a close reading of a single text) and explanation (that works with abstract models on a large groups of texts) I see an antithesis. Not just difference, but an either/or choice.

This said, I understand Eric Hayot's skepticism about how I formulate the antithesis at the end of the book: I am not happy with it either, and in the response to Prendergast's article I will try a different take, stressing the causal aspects of explanation, which are usually absent from interpretation. In a formula, interpretation posits a relationship between a meaning and another meaning, and explanation a (causal) relationship between an external force (or constraint) and one or more meanings. And then again, it may well be that the study of literature will always require, or be enriched by, both close reading and abstraction, interpretations and explanations; but this will amount to saying that literature requires two conceptually opposite approaches. Which is odd, and will make for some interesting speculation on why it should be so.

Finally, Tim Burke's "dumb luck" argument. (My favorite formulation comes from the extinction specialist David Raup: "Bad genes or bad luck?") It is certainly possible that dumb luck plays/played a much larger role than we imagine—probably larger and larger as we move back in history, and cultural products can disappear more easily. I will enlarge on this in my reply to Prendergast, but I may as well admit right away that every time I have studied competition, success, and failure, I have never found that luck played a major role (the only one exception I know: Austen's novels, despite having soldiers, include no reference to war, unlike most of her contemporaries, and the so-called "Hundred Years' Peace" that begun in 1815 rewarded her enormously for her choice: sheer external luck changing the world, and hence the expectations of generations of readers). (Needless to say, this is not the only ingredient in Austen's long-term success). But I admire Gould too, and would have liked to find instances of dumb luck. If anyone comes up with convincing examples, I'd love to see them.

And I do need to add, I don't ignore book history (it's the starting point of "Graphs," and about 50% of my last book), nor punctuated equilibria (which I first applied to literary history 20 years ago, and have used in the three books I have written since.)

Thanks again to all of you for the ideas and the challenges.

originally posted, January 15, 2006

http://www.thevalve.org/go/valve/article/moretti_responds_ii/

# ①⓪ Totality
# and
# the Genes of Literature

## JONATHAN GOODWIN

"Suppose at this juncture we were to state the blindingly obvious: that, whatever their other properties, literary texts do not possess genes" ("Graphs," 59). So begins the "Perils of Analogy" section of Christopher Prendergast's response to Moretti. Notwithstanding the *Paris Review* interviews, it does seem difficult to maintain that literature has genes. Does it have memes, however? Ideologemes? Maybe. And I will discuss metaphors of cultural transmission and evolutionary analogies in Moretti's argument.

The coherence of the meme concept is by no means obvious, and memes are not by any definition atomistic. Rukmini Nair suggests in *Narrative Gravity* that narrative is adapted to meme transmission (205). And the description of the Genre Evolution Project at the University of Michigan describes three versions of generic change: Leavis's great man, Lukács' great circumstance, and Barthes' great form. All are distinct from the biological model of generic evolution as envisioned by that project and also by Moretti. Biological evolution is mostly divergent (gene transfer and other poorly understood mechanisms being convergent) whereas cultural evolution is largely convergent with divergence resulting from the contingencies of imperfect transfer. Prendergast criticizes Moretti for overemphasizing divergence and suggests that it lends itself analogically to market-reification (61).

Moretti ends "Maps" with a quote from D'Arcy
Wentworth Thompson's *On Growth and Form*: "We rise from
a conception of form to an understanding of the forces which
gave rise to it [. . .] and in the comparison of kindred forms [.
. .] we discern the magnitude and the direction of the forces
which we have sufficed to convert the one form into the other"
(103). The phrase "diagram of forces in equilibrium" is elided
in the quote and appears in the last sentence of the chapter, mi-
nus "equilibrium" (Thompson, 1027). Thompson, translator of
Aristotle's biological treatises, knew better than to use the word
"entelechy" lightly; but I think it relevant here. A morphological
divergence is where a potentiality has become an actuality; and
the Aristotelian connotation of completion or perfection does
not necessarily entail triumphalism, as I think Prendergast suggests. So how to analyze the form of this governing force? Must
we suppose that literature is a machine?

I refer to the Galilean/Newtonian notion of the mechanism:

The modern scientific revolution, from Galileo, was
based on the thesis that the world is a great machine,
which could in principle be constructed by a master
artisan, a complex version of the clocks and other
intricate automata that fascinated the seventeenth
and eighteenth centuries, much as computers have
a provided a stimulus to thought and imagination
in recent years; the change of artifacts has limited
consequences for the basic issue as Alan Turing dem-
onstrated sixty years ago. (66)

Chomsky also observes that Newton refuted forever the
"mechanical philosophy"(67). All that is left scientifically is
the study of emergence in various forms.

Supposing that this is true of scientific theories about
the natural world, is it true of the study of literature? Can
imaginative literature be coherently described as a machine
constructed by a master artisan? How about the novel, spe-

cifically? Is the novel a species of theory-construction, of modeling? Does it explain the world by simplifying it, or does it contain, through extrinsic immanence, an image (or monad) of everything possible to be believed at the moment of its production? If not, perhaps the various genres at any given moment together form the well-rounded totality. "The individual work does not do justice to the genres by subsuming itself to them but rather through the conflict in which it long legitimated them, then engendered them, and ultimately canceled them" (Adorno, 208). You could apply this dialectic, *mutatis mutandis*, to organisms and species. Here's Moretti on the generic speciation-event (or extinction): "where a genre exhausts its potentialities—and the time comes to give the competitor a chance—when its inner form can no longer represent the most significant aspect of contemporary reality: at which point, either the genre betrays its form in the name of reality, thereby disintegrating, or it betrays reality in the name of form, becoming a 'dull epigone' indeed" ("Maps," 77 n8).

I am reminded here of Richard Goldschmidt's "hopeful monsters" from *The Material Basis of Evolution*, a concept and work reintroduced and recuperated to some extent by Stephen Jay Gould. Through developmental mechanisms, Goldschmidt argues, "a new type may emerge without accumulation of small steps" (251).Though not atomistic, combinable units, ideologemes may serve as an analyzable unit of developmental constraint. The word was probably first used by Bakhtin and/or Medvedev in *The Formal Method of Literary Scholarship*, and it appears most prominently in Bakhtin's "Discourse and the Novel" (333-35). Michael Holquist notes there that Bakhtin intends the term neutrally (429). The most influential discussion of ideologemes is in Jameson's *The Political Unconscious*:

An amphibious formulation whose essential structural characteristic may be described as its possibility to manifest itself either as a pseudoidea—a conceptual or belief system, an abstract value, an opinion or prejudice—or as a protonarrative, a kind of ultimate class fantasy about the "collective characters" which are the classes in opposition. (87)

Jameson further suggests that ideological analysis requires showing how the finished cultural product is a "complex work of transformation on the ultimate raw material which is the ideologeme in question" (87).

As Turing wrote in his influential paper about morphogenesis, "Most of an organism, most of the time, is developing from one pattern into another, rather than from homogeneity into a pattern" (71-2). Ideologemes are similar to Turing's morphogens in that they serve as developmental constraints on the production of a given text. It's worth supposing that narrative ecologies are optimally adapted to their historic environments and there is an inherently perfect transformation of experience in the act of narrative creation. The narrative property constructs abstract models, shares species-invariant characteristics, and integrates its individual variations into the totality of the social imagination: Coleridge's distinction of the primary and secondary imaginations ends by noting that the latter is "essentially vital" (167). This vitality of the secondary imagination allows the close reader to invent plausible historical claims, and distant readings of the state of the primary imagination discovers their context.

originally posted, January 24, 2006

http://www.thevalve.org/go/valve/article/totality_and_the_genes_of_literature/

## Works Cited

Adorno, Theodor W. *Aesthetic Theory*. ed. G. Adorno and R.Tiedemann. Trans. R. Hullot-Kentor. U of Minnesota Press, 1997.

Bakhtin, M. M. *The Dialogic Imagination*. Ed. M. Holquist. Trans. C. Emerson and M. Holquist. U of Texas Press, 1981.

Chomsky, Noam. *On Nature and Language*. Cambridge University Press, 2002.

Coleridge, Samuel Taylor. *Biographia Literaria*. Dent, 1956.

Goldschmidt, Richard B. *The Material Basis of Evolution*. 1940. Yale University Press, 1982.

Jameson, Fredric. *The Political Unconscious*. Cornell University Press, 1981.

Nair, Rukmini. *Narrative Gravity: Conversation, Cognition, and Culture*. Routledge, 2003.

Prendergast, Christopher. "Evolution and Literary History: A Response to Franco Moretti." *New Literary Review* 34 (July-August 2005): 40-62.

Thompson, D'Arcy Wentworth. *On Growth and Form*. Macmillan, 1943.

Turing, A. M. "The Chemical Basis of Morphogenesis." *Philosophical Transactions of the Royal Society of London. Series B, Biological Sciences*. 237.641, (Aug 14, 1952): 37-72.

# ①① Distant Reading Minds

## STEVEN BERLIN JOHNSON

Full disclosures first: Moretti is a friend, and was my advisor for several years during my grad school days at Columbia in the early nineties. I was there at the beginning of this project; I can still remember the slightly baffled silence the followed his announcement—over dinner with a half dozen grad students—that the future of literary criticism was going to lie in map-making. I spent an insane number of hours generating some of the first maps for him over the next year, using some now-obsolete cartography software that was, to say the least, not optimized for mapping narratives. So perhaps I'm biased by my fondness for Moretti—or by the desire not to think of all those hours generating maps as wasted ones—but I really do think that the two books that eventually emerged out of this research (*Atlas Of The European Novel* and *Graphs, Maps, Trees*) constitute a welcome and significant turning point in recent literary criticism. Just the density of ideas in *Graphs, Maps, Trees* alone is noteworthy; most scholars would have spun the analysis of genre cycles into an entire book, but Moretti gives you ten pages on it, and marches on to the next case study. It's exhilarating stuff, and I wouldn't have it any other way, but it does feel like we're going to be spending the next ten years unpacking some of these examples.

When Jonathan asked me to contribute to this discussion, he suggested one of the topics I might address would be the connection between my work in *Everything Bad Is Good*

*For You*, and Moretti's model in *Graphs, Maps, Trees*. As it happened, Moretti and I had just been exchanging a series of email messages remarking on how our thinking had developed along parallel lines since we both left Columbia. I talk about this a little in the Appendix to *Everything Bad*: the shift from a symbolic model to a systemic model. Most criticism ultimately involves, in one fashion or another, decoding the literary work to find the hidden meaning that lurks behind it. What form that meaning takes depends on the kind of critic you are: the genius of the author, the zeitgeist, the class struggle, the unconscious, the subaltern, *différance*. But the systemic approach to culture isn't looking for hidden meaning in the same way. This is how I described it in *Everything Bad*:

> My argument for the existence of the sleeper effect comes out of an assumption that the landscape of popular culture involves the clash of competing forces: the neurological appetites of the brain, the economics of the culture industry, changing technological platforms. The specific ways in which those forces collide plays a determining role in the type of popular culture we ultimately consume. The work of the critic, in this instance, is to diagram those forces, not decode them. Sometimes, for the sake of argument, I find it helpful to imagine culture as a kind of man-made weather system. Float a mass of warm, humid air over cold ocean water, and you'll create an environment in which fog will thrive. The fog doesn't appear because it somehow symbolically re-enacts the clash of warm air and cool water. Fog arrives instead as an emergent effect of that particular system and its internal dynamics. The same goes for culture....

Diagramming not decoding: you can hear the Moretti disciple loud and clear in that language. (You can also hear a little Manuel DeLanda, for what it's worth.) But the passage also points to an area that I hope Moretti will turn to next. You can't analyze the literary system purely from the bird's-eye-view of distant reading. You need to zoom in as much as you need to zoom out: all the way to the human brain itself. Consider this passage from *Graphs, Maps, Trees*:

> Everybody, from the first readers onwards, had noticed the country walks of *Our Village*; but no one had ever reflected on the circular pattern they project on the English countryside, because no one—in the absence of a map of the book—had ever managed to actually see it. (53)

Those readers might not have seen that circular pattern, but on some level, they must have perceived it; it must have shaped their experience of *Our Village* in some meaningful way. Otherwise, it's just a random pattern, formalist trivia, like discovering there are the same exact number of words beginning with "c" and "t" in the novel. The same goes for Conan Doyle and his rivals: the reading audience isn't consciously analyzing the formal properties of a stack of detective stories, and saying: "You know, I really like the ones with decodable clues." But nonetheless they're somehow processing those formal innovations, and building a sensibility around them, a preference for one configuration over the others.

So my question for Moretti is: how does this happen? How is the reader influenced by formal properties without being fully conscious of the influence? *Graphs, Maps, Trees* is silent on the question—understandably so, since he's got his hands full persuading us of the birds-eye-perspective. But a systemic theory has to work at all the relevant scales. All the science and empiricism of distant reading disappears when you get down to the level of the reader's mind: we're left with watered-down Freud: somehow the reader unconsciously digests the form, emphasis on "somehow." (I tried my hand at this approach for a few pages in *Everything Bad*—explaining how the formal architecture of reward and exploration in gaming connects to the brain's so-called "seeking circuitry.") In filling in the gap, I suspect that the cognitive sciences will be more relevant than evolutionary psychology, despite the fact that the Darwinian approach to literature has been attracting all the buzz lately. I'm less interested in where the brain's capacity for apprehending formal variation came from, and more interested in how it works. No doubt some these cognitive tools for apprehending literary form will turn out to be spandrels, or even exclusively the product of cultural training. That won't make those tools any less interesting. But we need to be able to talk with some rigor about how those semi-conscious assessments take hold in the brain—the same rigor that Moretti has applied to the system of literature itself. Right now all we have is superstition ...

originally posted, January 16, 2006
http://www.thevalve.org/go/valve/article/distant_reading_minds/

# ①② The Next Cigarette and a Modest Garnish

**JENNY DAVIDSON**

Something makes me yearn for certain brand-new books like a smoker plotting how to get her hands on the next cigarette, so that I will order Kazuo Ishiguro's latest at great expense from Amazon UK because of a release date three weeks earlier than in the US (worth every penny, by the way) or hit three different Cambridge bookstores in search of a non-sold-out copy of *On Beauty* in its first week of publication (perhaps not so satisfying an investment of time and money). I can't put my finger on exactly what produces that yearning in me, but it is far less likely to be prompted by a work of literary criticism than by a novel, and I was surprised to find myself coveting Franco Moretti's *Graphs, Maps, Trees: Abstract Models for a Literary History* to the point of being unwilling to wait for it to turn up at the library.

Indeed, the book has proved just as enjoyable as I expected, a highly stimulating read, though not perhaps as shocking as the flap copy suggests (in addition to the "heretical" counting and mapping there is a great deal of reading and thinking and arguing of a more familiar humanistic kind). What follows below: a few reflections on the book's style and methodology from the perspective of a reader at once seduced and rendered wary by a distinctive quality of Moretti's writing that Elif Batuman has labeled "the irresistible magnetism of the diabolical."

For me, the puzzle of the book concerns how seriously we're meant to take Moretti's grand flourishes in celebration of the quantitative. Moretti is of course aware of the self-contradictory aspects of his exercise. Following his quite wonderful bar graphs of the longevity of British novelistic genres between 1740 and 1915 (all the way from the courtship novel through the industrial novel and the school story to the New Woman novel and the Kailyard School), Moretti offers this admission in a footnote:

> See here how a quantitative history of literature is also a profoundly formalist one—especially at the beginning and at the end of the research process. At the end, for the reasons we have just seen; and at the beginning, because a formal concept is usually what makes quantification possible in the first place: since a series must be composed of homogeneous objects, a morphological category is needed—'novel', 'anti-Jacobin novel', 'comedy', etc.—to establish such homogeneity. (*GMT* 25 n. 14)

Is this a damaging admission, or a savvy one? The latter, I'd say, but it also only hints at my reservations about the claims of the chapter on "graphs."

As a scholar working in the field of eighteenth-century British literature and culture, I find Moretti's work around these questions fruitful but its distinctiveness or originality somewhat overstated. You don't have to be a heroic scientific pioneer and experimentalist to uncover the patterns in long-forgotten British novels of the eighteenth and nineteenth centuries; Ruth Perry's recent *Novel Relations*, for instance, reaps the rewards of a lifetime of reading eighteenth-century fiction to discern patterns (the rise of the novel of the second attachment, the trope of the *cri de sang*) that are as illuminating as Moretti's graphs about literary and social history. Moretti does not toil alone, in other words, and though his professional peers may lack his flair, they possess their own sorts of acumen; I'm thinking in particular of Gary Kelly's excellent work on the fiction of the 1790s and of Katie Trumpener and Claudia Johnson on the novels of Austen's generation and beyond. In a footnote to an earlier essay, "The Slaughterhouse of Literature," Moretti dismisses as socially insignificant the canon-bashing English professors who want simply to replace Jane Austen with Amelia Opie, but reading Opie's fiction alongside Austen's offers unusually clear and convincing evidence for why it's worth reading "minor" authors alongside their "major" contemporaries.[1] Elsewhere, in an essay called "Recovering Ellen Pickering," Poovey— prompted by the wording of an invitation from the British Women Writers Association—"gave some thought to the entire project of canon revision" and "decided to choose, virtually at random, a woman writer I had never heard of, read as much of her work as I could, then determine how, if at all, I could 'recover' this writer for modern scholars and students." And she includes some great diagrams! (Poovey's essay is followed by thoughtful responses from Margaret Homans and Jill Campbell, both well worth a look.)

Moretti isn't interested in chronicling these parallel developments in recent scholarship; nor does he acknowledge what is at the very least a broad family resemblance between his own work and that of another remarkable literary scholar, Wai Chee Dimock, who has also recently invoked Braudel in her call for the study of culture to become "planetary in scope."[2]

*Graphs, Maps, Trees* is a short manifesto, of course, a call for change rather than a survey of the field, so such exclusions are entirely understandable. More troubling for me is the undisputable fact that the vast quantitative-collaborative research project whose virtues Moretti propounds has something Pied-Piper-esque about it; without Moretti's own imagination and critical intelligence and deep knowledge of world literature driving it, doesn't the soul go out of the whole enterprise? We're speaking here about a scholar whose powerful intellect and imaginative scope have meant that he himself can make wonderful use of the human-graduate-student-equivalent of a commodity-cluster supercomputer; but without Moretti directing the whole enterprise, the prospects for communal enrichment come to look rather more bleak.

I don't dispute the striking insightfulness of Moretti's treatment of the distinction between village stories and provincial novels, in other words; he concludes in this case that villages and regions are homelands, whereas provinces are defined against a more desirable metropolitan center and are thus "'negative' entities, defined by what is not there," unmappable forms since "you cannot map what is not there" (53). And perhaps the most alluring instance of Moretti's diabolical charm comes in the sentence immediately following, which is both eminently reasonable and provocative to the point of being dandyish: "It happens, there are un-mappable forms (Christmas stories are another one, for different reasons), and these setbacks, disappointing at first, are actually the sign of a method still in touch with reality: geography is a useful tool, yes, but does not explain everything" (53). Oh, go ahead, do tell me why Christmas stories are unmappable! (I'm not being at all sarcastic; I really want to know . . . .) Might you be thinking in particular of "The Adventure of the Blue Carbuncle," the most famous Holmesian Christmas story, or does this sentence itself mimic the effect of the unreadable clues of Conan Doyle and his contemporaries, providing something that looks awfully like a clue but resists interpretation because of an absence of meaningful context?

Moretti is surely poking a bit of fun at himself here, writing in a style close to self-parody, as when he offers a flippant aside right after that modest disclaimer about geography's failure to explain everything ("For that, we have astrology and 'Theory'"). But this is Moretti's own personal insightfulness, not a blueprint for cultural development; despite the easy availability of quantitative techniques, in other words, it's hard for me to think of a school of literary interpretation less suited to reproduction on a mass scale.

I take the richest payoff here in terms of literary history, then, to be an insight that has also been arrived at elsewhere and by other routes. The "real content of the controversy", Moretti says, "is our very idea of culture":

> Because if the basic mechanism of change is that of divergence, then cultural history is bound to be random, full of false starts, and profoundly path-dependent: a direction, once taken, can seldom be reversed, and culture hardens into a true 'second nature'—hardly a benign metaphor. If, on the other hand, the basic mechanism is that of convergence, change will be frequent, fast, deliberate, reversible: culture becomes more plastic, more human, if you wish. But as human history is so seldom human, this is perhaps not the strongest of arguments. (81)

The relationship between trees and contingency (and the chapter on "Trees," with its treatment of the clue in the detective story of Conan Doyle's time, seems to me by far the most interesting) is something about which Moretti is even more explicit in an earlier essay, discussing the same idea. There he calls the failure of Conan Doyle's rivals—and indeed of the creator of Sherlock Holmes himself—to explore the full literary potential of the clue "a good instance of the rigidity of literary evolution":

> you only learn once; then you are stuck. You learn, so it's culture, not nature: but it's a culture which is as unyielding as DNA. And the consequence of this is that literary changes don't occur slowly, piling up one small improvement upon another: they are abrupt, structural, and leave very little room for transitional forms. ("Slaughterhouse," 222)

The tree's payoff, in other words, mainly concerns contingency: "What the tree says is that literary history could be different from what it is" ("Slaughterhouse," 227). Interesting, true; but didn't we know that already? And culture can be as deterministic as nature, no surprise to Montesquieu and the eighteenth-century climate theorists (or for that matter to William James).

In the book's version of the "Trees" piece, Moretti's discussion of the clue segues into a really wonderful treatment of "the still numerous 'ways of being alive' discovered between 1800 and 2000 by that great narrative device known as 'free indirect style'" (81). This, for me, was the most thought-provoking part of the discussion and yet also the one that bore the least resemblance to the polemical version of "distant reading" and looked most like good old-fashioned twentieth-century literary criticism, with a kind of geographical expansiveness that owes more to earlier generations of scholars of comparative literature than to recent work in the life sciences. Moretti's figure 33, "Free indirect style in modern narrative, 1800-2000," has this legend below: "This figure reflects work in progress, and is therefore quite tentative, especially in the case of non-European literatures, and of the diachronic span of the various branches" (84). But isn't this just a way of fancying-up, so to speak, the insights of Moretti's critical prose, itself a supple and powerful enough tool to operate diagramless? We don't need this "schematic visualization" (82); Moretti's thoughts on Austen and Flaubert and Dostoevsky-by-way-of-Bakhtin are the meat here, the figure possibly just a modish garnish to be set aside before tucking into the main dish.

originally posted, January 17, 2006

http://www.thevalve.org/go/valve/article/the_next_cigarette_and_a_modest_
garnish/

## Works Cited

Dimock, Wai Chee. "Genre as World System: Epic and Novel on Four Continents." *Narrative* 14.1 (2006): 85-101.

—. "Planetary Time and Global Translation: 'Context' in Literary Studies." *Common Knowledge* 9.3 (2003): 488-507.

Moretti, Franco. "The Slaughterhouse of Literature." *Modern Language Quarterly* 61.1 (2000): 207-27.

Poovey, Mary. "Recovering Ellen Pickering." *Yale Journal of Criticism* 13.2 (2000): 437-52.

## Notes

1   Franco Moretti, "The Slaughterhouse of Literature," *Modern Language Quarterly* 61:1 (2000): 207-27; 209 n. 3.

2   The piece is "Planetary Time and Global Translation: 'Context' in Literary Studies," p. 488. See also the full elaboration of this argument in her wonderful recent essay, "Genre as World System: Epic and Novel on Four Continents" which includes a discussion of Moretti's "distant reading," 90-91.

# ①③ Judging Books by Their Covers
## - or -
## Chance Favors the Prepared Meme

### JOHN HOLBO

In "Trees," Moretti speculates about literary 'character' traits that may confer 'evolutionary advantage'. A candidate case: the clue as detective fiction device [see figure 3, p. 49]. Moretti sketches a tree. I'll quote the expository accompaniment:

> Two things were immediately clear: the 'formal' fact that several of Doyle's rivals (those on the left) did not use clues—and the 'historical' fact that they were all forgotten. It is a good illustration of what the literary market is like: ruthless competition—hinging on form. Readers discover that they like a certain device, and if a story doesn't seem to include it, they simply don't read it (and the story becomes extinct). This pressure of cultural selection probably explains the second branching of the tree, where clues are present, but serve no real function: as in 'Race with the Sun', for instance, where a clue reveals to the hero that the drug is in the third cup of coffee, and then, when he is offered the third cup, he actually drinks it. Which is indeed 'perplexing & unintelligible', and the only possible explanation is that these writers realized that

clues were popular, and tried to smuggle them into their stories—but hadn't really understood how clues worked, and so didn't use them very well.

Let me jump a paragraph to an objection Moretti tries to answer. The tree in question assumes morphology is key. "But why should form be the decisive reason for survival? Why not social privilege instead—the fact that Doyle was writing for a well-established magazine and his rivals were not?" Moretti tries to solve for this variable by establishing that Doyle's choice perch in *Strand Magazine* was shared by others. Not only that, there was more 'genetic diversity' just in *Strand* than even fig. 3 suggests (see fig. 4).

Very interesting, but let's step back up into the above paragraph and run a variant objection. "Readers discover that they like a certain device, and if a story doesn't seem to include it, they simply don't read it (and the story becomes extinct)." The problem is: Moretti's tree plots actual inclusions, not seeming ones. And anyway: how does a story set about *seeming* to include something before you've actually read it?

You sell books to people who haven't read them yet, hence who don't *know* what they contain. On the other hand, Doyle's *longue durée* endurance run is plausibly due in large part to his stories' winning forms: people like clues, especially those who are fans of the genre of mystery stories. (Yes, there's certainly no danger of it turning out that people *don't* like clues. So what are we hoping to learn that we didn't know already?)

Let's be a bit artificial and say the literary competition takes place in two stages: first, a book will be 'judged by its cover', and must win; if it wins, it gets the chance to be widely judged for what is between its covers. If it wins again, it 'avoids extinction', i.e. becomes a classic (or at least doesn't flash in the pan.)

Just yesterday Jenny Davidson began her post by writing: "Something makes me yearn for certain brand-new books like a smoker plotting how to get her hands on the next cigarette ... I can't put my finger on exactly what produces that yearning in me ..." And just yesterday I linked to Art Spiegelman's tale of first love. "She was a paperback cover girl and I couldn't keep my hands off her." I think we're all acquainted with some such experience of *seeming*. It isn't pure black arts of marketing, I trust. On the other hand, there are such arts. A few weeks ago [Wednesday 28 December 2005] the *Guardian* ran a piece about statisticians trying to predict bestsellers not from covers but titles:

> The team of three statisticians, helped by programmers, studied 54 years of fiction number ones in the *New York Times* and the 100 favourite novels in the BBC's Big Read poll.
>
> Comparing these with a control group of less successful novels by the same authors, they found that the winning books had three common features; they had metaphorical, or figurative titles instead of literal ones; the first word was a pronoun, a verb, an adjective or a greeting; and their grammar patterns took the form either of a possessive case with a noun, or of an adjective and noun or of the words The ... of ...
>
> By this formula the most perfect titles were Agatha Christies' last thriller *Sleeping Murder* (1976) and Philip Pullman's *His Dark Materials*, both with 83% marks. The poorest was Patricia Cornwell's thriller *Cause of Death*, with 9%.
>
> British authors produced the highest-scoring titles in both studies. John Le Carre was the most consistent with *Smiley's People*, *The Spy Who Came in From the Cold*, *The Tailor of Panama* and others.
>
> Dr Winkler said: "When we tested our model on 700 titles published over 50 years, it correctly predicted whether a book was a bestseller or not for nearly 70% of cases. This is 40% better than random guesswork. It is far from perfect but given the nature

of the data and the way tastes change 70% accuracy is surprisingly good."

They missed *The Da Vinci Code* and *Harry Potter*. Still, what does Moretti have to say about this sort of thing? (I don't mean to be insulting, suggesting Moretti has never considered that people read after they buy, that there is such a thing as marketing, etc. I just wonder what he has to say about it.)

And yes, obviously my two-stage process is not tidy. Your book needs to be consistently selected to get read. This isn't just a matter of an eye-catchy cover, or snappy title. It's also a matter of getting an editor to read you, then select you for prominent placement to be read by many others. It's a matter of opinion-formers—'coolhunters', first adopters, reviewers, literary cliques, what shelf it gets shelved on, what genre tag gets attached to it, what authors become 'brand names'. Oprah. Most of this activity indeed has to do with books actually being read, and winning the 'ruthless competition' to some degree as Moretti supposes: editors, reviewers, early adopters, Oprah, have to like the form of your book (it's got clues!) Still, in laying stress on the morphology of what's between the covers, Moretti risks assuming efficiency in the diffusion of information about morphology. We have an efficient literary market hypothesis. I don't see a strong reason for believing in this efficiency.

And be it noted: the evolutionary analogies may still pan out, even if my skepticism is warranted (so we are not really arguing about whether we should go on talking about evolution, or the market-place.) I might seem to be saying: you *can* judge a book by its cover, and we do. But natural selection is not such an idle browser: you can't judge, um, a beetle by its carapace. Ergo, I am distinguishing the lazy reading styles/ purchasing practices of humans from Mother Nature's more rigorous critical practices. But this is wrong. You *can* judge a beetle by its cover: red means poison (keep away!) Covers are as adaptive in nature, red in tooth and claw, as on the bookrack, red in ripped bodices and teeth and claws and other popular offerings. And for similar reasons. It is often advantageous to convey a strong sense of what's inside.

At this point, let me turn to the luck argument. Moretti responds to Tim Burke:

> It is certainly possible that dumb luck plays/played a much larger role than we imagine—probably larger and larger as we move back in history, and cultural products can disappear more easily. I will enlarge on this in my reply to Prendergast, but I may as well admit right away that every time I have studied competition, success, and failure, I have never found that luck played a major role (the only one exception I know: Austen's novels, despite having soldiers, include no reference to war, unlike most of her contemporaries, and the so-called "Hundred Years' Peace" that begun in 1815 rewarded her enormously for her choice: sheer external luck changing the world, and hence the expectations of generations of readers.) (Needless to say, this is not the only ingredient in Austen's long-term success). But I admire Gould too, and would have liked to find instances of dumb luck. If anyone comes up with convincing examples, I'd love to see them.

Rather than pretend to some dataset at my fingertips [see postscript for the dataset that turned up later] let me dogmatically opine that J.K. Rowling is *lucky*. She's good, not *that* good. At some point something tipped. Her books came to occupy an oddly favorable position, which cascaded into favor upon favor. Straining a bit, you might say that what you have here is mild cultural 'lock-in', on the model of the 'lock-in' Microsoft has enjoyed—except that everyone *likes* Harry.

Harry Potter is a cultural operating system unto himself. People read Harry because otherwise they wouldn't know what's going on when everyone else is talking about Harry. There are social benefits to reading Harry and social costs of not doing so, for people who are not otherwise plugged into any systems of literary reputation (snobbish or sensitive or otherwise). And don't forget plain old-fashioned brand name recognition. But it could have been a different author whose works lucked into that role. Or, more likely, no author. (Who thinks it was necessary that any literary success on this scale was inevitably emergent at just this juncture in history?)

A large thesis, yes. But significant because, in denying 'luck' in the study of "competition, success, and failure" Moretti seems committed to denying the possibility of things we *know* happen in, say, business. (Don't we?)

It seems to me obvious that Rowling is not a unique case, merely an extreme one. Many authors occupy cultural niches that others might occupy but don't happen to. On the other hand, is it right to call this 'luck'? Rowling is a lucky woman. But 'dumb luck' may suggest there is no rational explanation, which is something else. This gets us back to Burke:

> But as for how Doyle's stories set the conventions of a genre and others die, are forgotten, wither, some of that might be simply termed "dumb luck," that the precise location at which crystallization of a genre occurs in a moment where many nascent forms of the genre are present is about the accidents of readership, of circulation, of publication, of imitation, that there is no deeper explanation that needs to cite how Doyle's particular formulation of the genre more precisely satisfied or represented the desires of a reading public, or how his ability as a writer was more precisely distinguished from any other. I'm echoing Gould's *Wonderful Life* here very consciously.

Which is it? No explanation? Or we can't know it? (Because it's unreconstructable, or just wouldn't exhibit enough interest?) I push the point because it seems plausible that the explanation in Doyle's case might be that Holmes got famous through a series of lucky breaks (such as Tim Burke is thinking of); yet these breaks can only be understood with reference to certain 'morphological' features, in Moretti's sense. Chance favors the prepared meme.

## Postscript

When I wrote the original version of this piece, in 2006, there was indeed (to my knowledge) no dataset to test any form of the 'lucky break' hypothesis in rigorous fashion. If you pressed reset, then let it play out again, would Harry Potter come out on top again? Alas, the actual world lacks a reset button (or perhaps that's a good thing, at least for nonscientific purposes; but scientifically inconvenient.) But in 2007, just such a data set was ingeniously collected. Experimenters at Columbia University—Matthew Salganik, Peter Dodds, and Duncan Watts—set up MusicLab, an online environment consisting of 'worlds' in which participants rate and download songs by (unknown) bands. The experimenters constructed 'independent' and 'social influence' worlds. In the former, participants could see only song titles and band names (randomly ordered); in social influence worlds songs were ranked according to participants' ratings (1 to 5 stars) and download counts were visible as well. In two social influence worlds, this social information was falsified—inverted, to be exact. The highest-rated song appeared to be the lowest-rated, and vice versa.

As the title of a paper by the experimenters suggests—"Leading the Herd Astray: An Experimental Study of Self-fulfilling Prophecies in an Artificial Cultural Market"—the experiment was devised to test not Moretti's hypothesis but its approximate opposite: namely, the notion that social influence is *all*. So, for example, a song falsely identified as popular will become popular—self-fulfilling prophecy. Obviously, Moretti's skepticism about the role of luck is likewise testable in such an environment. (I acknowledge that Moretti is not dogmatic in his claims about the role of luck, so it would not be fair to say his view is falsifiable by such an experiment. Still, he clearly has strong personal opinions that may—and will—be challenged by the likes of MusicLab.)

A quick note: it is misleading to continue using terms like 'luck' and 'chance'. We are actually talking about forms of social influence. Let's review how we've gotten a bit off-track: even if it *is* luck in the Harry Potter case, in the sense that no one has any story to tell about an ingenious marketing scheme that seeded the famous series' popularity, it certainly is not the case that *all* advantageous social/cultural positioning/influence is due to luck.

What I am thinking about, when I talk 'luck' in my piece, is mostly the power of path dependence; of initial advantage (due to chance or any other source, social or otherwise) cascading to dramatic effect. This is what Robert Merton calls (and Malcolm Gladwell has popularized as) 'the Matthew effect': "for unto everyone that hath shall be given, and he shall have abundance. But from him that hath not shall be taken away even that which he hath" (25:29). It is also the Paris Hilton effect: famous for being famous. Initial advantage—small thing—*can* be sheer luck. Something snowballed for Harry Potter, then a self-reinforcing social-influence feedback loop got established (plausibly). But the fact that what seeded Harry's snowball, initially, may have been some snowflake of dumb luck is not essential to the shape of the question, or to the discovery of any answer. So what does the answer turn out to be, insofar as the Music Lab experiment discovers any?

Unsurprisingly (I would say) the pure, self-fulfilling prophecy hypothesis is not borne out. Neither is any pure quality-will-out hypothesis, however (without which the proposition that luck is not a significant factor earns a serious question mark.) Moretti would be gratified to learn that the top quality song in the independent world also reached the top in the basic social influence world; and, even when falsely accused of being low quality in inverted social influence worlds, was on-track to regain its top spot (although the experiment ended before this result was attained, if ever it would have been.) But the number two song's standing was not similarly immune to social influence and manipulation. In general, there was a great deal of variation, across worlds, pointing to the power of social influence, also to the power of path dependence. Small things, early on, make a big difference in the end. So luck *does* end up playing a big role. These worlds, despite being identical at the level of the features of the aesthetic objects they contain, diverge significantly. And, frankly, it would be incredible if, in the real world, these effects were *less*, rather than more, than in this toy experimental environment. (The interested reader should review the experimenters' own conclusions, and their more quantitatively precise statements of their results.)

What lesson should Moretti take from this?

He is not refuted, since (to repeat) he does not commit himself categorically to any specific, falsifiable proposition about the non-role of luck (or social influence); but he should be a bit chastened. "I may as well admit right away that every time I have studied competition, success, and failure, I have never found that luck played a major role." This may be true, as a report of personal experience But it will not do. Moretti's mindset seems to be this: he can see a potential variable he cannot see how to control for. He is, in effect, hoping he can do without controlling it. Unfortunately, it does not seem he can really be right.

On the other hand, it hardly seems impossible to envision (very empirically ambitious, to be sure) attempts to study the sorts of things Moretti studies and the sorts of things the MusicLab experimenters study; the two approaches really ought to be complementary, even if they do challenge each other's assumptions at points.

Consider this. The Music Lab experimenters' incidental reflections on the nature of aesthetic quality do not mar their social psychological experimental designs, nor do they invalidate their reasoning to various conclusions. Still, their reflections are so innocent I cannot help suspecting tongues in cheeks (at least I hope they are, a little bit):

> An obvious explanation for the failure of the inversion to lock in [i.e. popular songs falsely identified as unpopular recover their rank somewhat, and unpopular songs false identified and popular sink down in the ranks somewhat] is that the songs themselves were of different quality, and that these differences were more salient than the perception of popularity. Previous theoretical work by economists has indeed emphasized the importance of intrinsic quality on outcomes (Rosen 1981), and attempts have been made to measure the quality of cultural products (Hamlen Jr. 1991; Krueger 2005). Unfortunately, no generally agreed upon measure of quality exists, in large part because quality is largely, if not completely, a social construction (Gans 1974; Becker 1982; Bourdieu 1984; DiMaggio 1987; Cutting 2003; Frith 2004). (Salganik, Watts, 349)

I do not think it was necessary for these authors, in this particular paper, to survey the history of ideas about art, culture, aesthetic judgment, and critical consensus. But, having decided to go down that line, it was incumbent on them to go further; to take note that the literature stretches back before 1981, to say the least, and beyond the economics department.

History of aesthetics and art criticism, anyone? (David Hume, at least? Adam Smith read him, after all.)

Also, the proposition that 'quality is largely, if not completely, a social construction'—is simply not the sort of thing one can assume, or even claim as weakly supported by any existing body of data. Not because there is evidence it is false, merely because the claim is ambiguous and vague. We don't know what is being claimed. But the truth concerning the area being blanketed by this claim is quite important, potentially. At least it is interesting.

Before I take another step, let me say that I may be about to protest too much: I don't think that anyone proposing Moretti-esque studies, regarding music (or any other cultural products), would in fact be unreasonably dismissed by the MusicLab experimenters. If someone proposed investigating features of the songs from the MusicLab experiment set; if investigators found relations or connections, intriguing patterns, I am sure the MusicLab experimenters would be quick enough to see this line might be worthwhile. Nevertheless, this 'socially constructed' line has a tendency to plow through the interest of what Moretti does in conceptually incoherent fashion. Let me try to clear that up. (Even if the confusion would not cause trouble, in practice—which it might not—it will be nice to have some theoretical sense of how projects like Moretti's, and these MusicLab investigators, might interlock, conceptually.)

The MusicLab experimenters are tending to assume that value can only be measured as a function of preference; preference is a feature of audiences, not art works. This might make it seem that you can only study value (in this sense) by studying audiences, as opposed to art works, which is pretty much what MusicLab does. (For experimental purposes, the songs in their set might as well be black boxes.) But, in a sense, this is just false: many musicological features whose relations to MusicLab results might be worth investigation (length, beats-per-minute, instrumentation, even style) are non-socially constructed, on any plausible account of what 'social-constructed' means. (Even style? You can't make something a sonata just by saying it is one. It has to have the right features.) You can study all that, how various features song features are correlated with other features, how all that is correlated with preferences and also perhaps how it is correlated with susceptibility to or immunity to social influence. (I'm not saying I know there would be interesting results. But it would be perfectly possible to check for them, empirically.)

Even if 'fast songs are good songs' is only true in the sense that a solid democratic bloc reports that it *likes* fast songs (which begs the question against certain competing accounts of 'value', no doubt, but that is fine so long as you are clear about it); still, studying aesthetic values, in this subjectivist sense, does not entail the exclusive study of *subjects*, as opposed to *works*; because beats per minute is not a matter of what anyone thinks, let alone what anyone prefers. So: you look to preferences to see which properties of a song are interesting, for aesthetic study purposes. (It turns out that tempo is important. Surely this will be the case.) But then the properties that show up as valuable (or as correlated with values, if you are absolutely insistent on keeping value in the eye of the beholder) really are properties *of the song*. They can be investigated to a considerable extent quite independently of anything except the songs themselves. Again, I doubt anyone would really make this mistake in practice. But these authors may do so in theory, so it's worth pointing out where the fallacy slips in.

Let's shift, hypothetically, to MysteryLab, where Moretti has run fresh experiments. There isn't much point in me making up results, although I feel confident that they would not be so different from the MusicLab results. Pace Moretti, social influence and chance would play a significant role. (Until someone does it, of course, Moretti—and you, too—are free to keep whatever faith about the role of luck that you like.) I would emphasize only that it is obviously not necessary to treat art objects themselves as black boxes, as it were, for purposes of experimental design. It is not even too late, in the MusicLab case, to undertake a Morettiesque study of the features of the works themselves. The songs still exist, from which you could generate data about song features. It would be interesting to see what emerged, I think.

originally posted January 18, 2006<br>
http://www.thevalve.org/go/valve/article/judging_books_by_their_covers_or_<br>
chance_favors_the_prepared_meme/

## Works Cited

Salganik, Matthew and Duncan Watts, "Leading the Herd Astray: An Experimental Study of Self-fulfilling Prophecies in an Artificial Cultural Market," *Social Psychology Quarterly* 71, 4 (2008): 338-355.

# ①④ Moretti
# Responds (III)

**FRANCO MORETTI**

First, public thanks to Bob O'Hara—years ago I read his "Homage to Clio," and it helped me think about evolution and historiography. I have started reading some more of his work this morning, and look forward to the rest.

Tim Burke's new version of the 'dumb luck' idea makes much more sense to me, especially in John Holbo's version that "luck favors the prepared meme." Here, a morphological tree allows to recapture, not the luck exactly, but at least the initial proximity between the winner and the rivals—a proximity that market mechanisms quickly magnify into a galactic gap. In this sense, there is a continuity between the morphological argument (that establishes the—often tiny—difference in initial conditions) and the social one (that explores the path dependency created by, in our case, literary markets). Going back to the issue of luck, every lock-in is a piece of luck [Doyle may have deserved to fare better, but not *that much* better!] But if the mechanism behind "social" luck is known (it a feedback loop, as Arthur and others have shown), it remains to be seen what is the mechanism behind "morphological" luck.

Steven Johnson's question—How is the reader influenced by formal properties without being fully conscious of the influence?—is similar to Bill Benzon's "how is it that the world makes its way into the mind there to be transformed into texts?" Once more, I wish I knew an answer. What I did in the book was to leave a black box in the explanatory chain: given how the text is made, and given the success decreed by its readers, there must be a passage in between where certain formal properties are perceived by those who are reading, even though we have no actual evidence that the latter are aware of them. "There must be": that's the black box. One should open it up, and explain how it works. When I will start studying a solution, I think I'll follow Steven's advice, and assume that the cognitive sciences will be more relevant than evolutionary psychology.

Jenny Davidson finds the project "Pied-Piper-esque," because too dependent on my own knowledge: without which, she writes, "doesn't the soul go out of the whole enterprise?" Thanks for the kind words, but if you remove the person who has done most of the work, doesn't the soul go out of *any* enterprise?

Sociological coda. As for my having at my disposal "the human-graduate-student-equivalent of a commodity-cluster supercomputer," not to mention the hints by John Emerson about grad students voting en bloc at the MLA—I have been teaching in the US for 15 years, and have never been a member of the MLA, so that's unlikely. As for grad students doing the primary work on which I later build castles in the air, this has happened a few times—but much more often in the opposite direction, with me gathering the primary data, and placing them at the disposal of students or readers. [Incidentally, it's amazing how few people are willing to work on data that you have collected. Don't ask me why.] Grad students are in general wary of projects like *Graphs, Maps, Trees*. They realize they are very time-consuming, as one may work for weeks gathering data that reveal nothing. In my situation, I can afford the waste [although I hate it], but they can't. And then, they are a lot less sure than some contributors to The

Valve that this will be a significant trend in literary studies. Conclusion: of the many students who work with me only one in five, maybe one in ten, works along the lines of my last book. Professionally, this is bad for me [my research needs more data, gathered by different minds, etc]. leaves my students and myself with our own paths and intellectual personalities.

originally posted, January 19, 2006
http://www.thevalve.org/go/valve/article/moretti_responds_iii/

# ①⑤ A Few Quibbles about Moretti's Graphs, Maps, Trees

## SEAN MCCANN

I love *Graphs, Maps, and Trees*. Who couldn't? If you're not dazzled by the erudition and the data set, how could you fail to find instruction and delight in the nimbleness of Moretti's mind and the brio of his prose? But, love it though I do, like Matt, Ray, and Jenny Davidson, I'm not so sure that GMT can really "delineate a transformation in the study of literature" as Moretti suggests (*NLR* 67). (On the "Maps" technique, let me recommend another superb precursor, Carlo Rotella's *October Cities*.) I applaud Moretti's remarkable commitment to research. I admire his interest in "explanation" as against "interpretation" (even if I'm not sure the distinction finally holds up). I'm attracted to his emphasis on "devices and genres; not texts." And I welcome his enthusiasm for analogies and examples drawn from all sorts of disciplines arguably related to literary scholarship. I'm still more taken by his intellectual seriousness and his evident appreciation for the artfulness of literary creativity. But looking at the essays in combination and considering some of the many different sources of insight I think they combine, I don't see a new methodology for literary study so much as a sterling example of comparative literary scholarship at its most inspired—*à la* Auerbach, Spitzer, Bakhtin. Here's an unscientific prediction. There will be no school of Moretti, because only Moretti will prove able to do what's on display here.

A few minor thoughts about why that might be so.

First of all, I think it should be noted that, fruitful though it clearly is, the "quantitative" angle could easily become misleading. It's wonderful to see the graphs and to get a sense of the vast range of material that still needs to be discovered and understood. But as Moretti notes ("Graphs" 72), all this is just data until hypotheses are generated. And it's in the hypotheses (produced, by the way, via "interpretation") that Moretti's most serious commitments and their potential limits standout.

The real interest, as Moretti indicates throughout, is not so much in quantification as in the end it serves— "comparative morphology" ("Trees" 62). The central argument of the three essays, as I read them, is that literary form is a record of (highly various) forces that can be discovered by the scrupulous reader (102). Among the places, Moretti puts this most clearly is a passage in "Maps." It deserves to be, I think, a stunner of a line:

Deducing from the *form* of the object, the *forces* that have been at work: this is the most elegant definition ever of what literary sociology should be. (97)

Perhaps I'm over-reading, but "deducing" brought me up short. I would have said that one fundamental implication of Moretti's research program is that it should hold out little hope for deducing at all. If you're gathering information on the publication history of the novel, then presumably there is no object to investigate, only (to use the evolutionary terminology Moretti introduces) population groups. And, if I understand correctly, short of molecular biology, the only way to understand population groups is via induction. With the history of publishing and reading, too, that induction should arguably range over a pretty wide span of territory—including (to take up some points mentioned by Timothy Burke and John Holbo) whatever can be gathered about readers, industries, markets, mediators, and institutions.

Moretti leaves most of that material aside here, along with some of the existing scholarship (genre theory, as Matt notes, but also, e.g., publishing and literacy history) that emphasizes different factors than he places at the fore. In other words, it's not only pedantry to pause at the deduction thing. As he was in the exhilarating early essays collected in *Signs Taken for Wonders*, Moretti remains form-centric. And, while he makes that approach highly rewarding indeed, it rests on some basic assumptions whose unargued status (and, perhaps, inconsistencies) leave GMT less a portent of a new approach to cultural history than a brilliant example of literary criticism at its best.

1) The most striking of those assumptions, indicated in "Graphs," is the notion adopted from Russian formalism that literary genres function to "represent the most significant aspects of contemporary reality" (77, n.8). Combining Shklovsky with Kuhn, Moretti suggests that genres resemble scientific paradigms and organize the perception of reality in productive but inevitably limited ways. I find this an intuitively appealing notion, but I think you've got to acknowledge that it remains unproven and probably unprovable. It's not hard, for example, to consider other possible functions served by genres—preserving the shared values of a culture, say, or providing entertainment value. Could such functions be consistent with the representation of "reality"? Quite possibly, but it can take some creative interpretation to make the case. (Why did the movie musical flourish and decline? Was it really the genre's ability to represent reality?)

2) That first assumption, which reads form as a way to organize the perception of reality sits alongside a second assumption, with which it may be, but I think isn't necessarily consistent. This is the view expressed in the Conan Doyle section of "Trees" that sees the diversity, success, and failure of literary forms as the product of market selection. The selecting agent here, of course, is not the pressure of changing historical reality itself, but the preferences of a popular readership. (It's possible to argue, of course, that readers will select for forms that represent reality well, but that doesn't follow inevitably.)

3) Finally, the emphasis on reader selection runs up against the claim in the latter part of "Trees," with its fascinating discussion of free indirect discourse, that history and social geography determine the use of literary techniques—a suggestion that more closely resembles the assumption noted in "Graphs."

Although I think it interferes with some of the elegance of Moretti's argument, I also believe that it's a very good thing that the latter part of "Trees" reintroduces the emphasis on social geography emphasized by "Maps." Otherwise, the discussion of Conan Doyle could be taken to imply that Moretti's method depends on a unidimensional model of the literary market. Discussing the rise of the detective story, Moretti suggests that what survives is just what worked and what readers liked—so that the sale of pop fiction appears to function as something like an efficient market. ("What the literary market is like: literary competition—hinging on form. Readers discover that they like a certain device, and if a story doesn't seem to include it, they simply don't read it (and the story becomes extinct)" (48).) But, striking though this particular case study is, that impression will probably only work with a fairly narrow example—and one where low-cost entertainment lit is at the fore. With cheap, mass circulation entertainment, it makes sense to assume that consumer preference probably shapes the production and popularity of literary fashion most directly. Needless to say, however, not all literature is only a consumer good. Just to choose some minor complications, some of it also serves pedagogical, ideological, and status purposes. And those complications on the reception side are mirrored on the production side. Moretti quickly considers and dismisses (with one striking, but still quite limited piece of data) the role of status in influencing the chances of literary success. But surely the status battles of artists are a major engine of modern creativity, and the success they crave is not only secured by readership in numbers.

Of course, Moretti doesn't need to take the full range of these complications into account in order to have fascinating things to say. But I think they cast some doubt on the analogy of literary scholarship to scientific research. One further example. Toward the end of "Trees" Moretti emphasizes the "the dependence of morphological novelty on spatial discontinuity," drawing an implicit analogy to evolutionary speciation (62). But, if I understand right, the essay combines two, not necessarily fully overlapping senses of environment: the market in which products compete for reader attention (emphasized in the discussion of Doyle); and the social world they claim to represent (emphasized in the discussion of free indirect discourse). Especially when Moretti discusses Gabriel Garcia Márquez—surely a world novelist with an international market by the time he wrote Patriarch—it seems clear that these two kinds of environment differ and don't necessarily overlap. Only the first really works with the evolutionary analogy.

Personally, I won't be much disappointed if literary scholarship never really resembles scientific investigation. I wish we all were as good as Moretti and shared his seriousness and creativity. But I'm not sure a more rational form of literary history is needed. At one point in "Trees" Moretti makes a rather striking comment about one reason why he thinks otherwise. The comment comes in the course of Moretti's disagreement with Alfred Kroeber about whether the evolution of biological species differs from the evolution of cultural forms. Kroeber thinks there is a fundamental difference and that it's evident in the convergence, as well as divergence, of cultural forms. Moretti disagrees and raises the stakes, saying "the real content of the controversy, not technical at all, is our very idea of culture." If we stress divergence:

> then cultural history is bound to be random, full of false starts, and profoundly path dependent.... If, on the other hand, the basic mechanism is that of convergence, change will be frequent, fast, deliberate, reversible: culture becomes more plastic, more human if you wish. But as human history is seldom so human, this is perhaps not the strongest of arguments. (55-56)

Perhaps not. But that last witticism isn't much of an argument either and, if I understand correctly, doesn't really address Kroeber's contention at all. (Pointing out the human agency in unnatural selection doesn't necessarily imply a belief that history is humane.) More seriously, aren't we posed with a false choice here? I'm way out of my depth with this stuff, but I would have thought that, if we take the analogy to evolutionary biology seriously, then neither convergence nor divergence would count as a "basic mechanism." Wouldn't both merely be the effects of random variation and selection?

If that's so, Moretti presents us with a needless conflict, and one that suggests that a part of the motivation for his transformation of literary study may be the long-standing desire to purge culture of its humanist legacies. I'm sympathetic to that goal in part, but I don't think it's really required for a meaningful cultural history.

originally posted, January 19, 2006
http://www.thevalve.org/go/valve/article/human_not_so_human/

## Works Cited

Rotella, Carlo. *October Cities: The Redevelopment of Urban Literature.* University of California Press, 1998.

# ①⑥ Graphs, Trees, Materialism, Fishing

## COSMA SHALIZI

A few years ago, I wrote a review of Moretti's *Atlas of the European Novel*, in which I presumed to tell him how to go about his business. When he ran across it, his reaction was not (as mine would've been, had our situation been reversed) to tell me where to get off, but to invite me to a workshop he was organizing at Stanford on new interdisciplinary work on the novel—its motto, the quotation from Brecht about "questions that appear to us completely unsolved," is recycled for this book —where I had a great time. Reading these essays as they came out in *New Left Review*, I enjoyed them intensely, and recall thinking that Moretti could hardly have done a better job of appealing to my prejudices if he'd tried. (Said prejudices are those of someone almost equally fond of *The Extended Phenotype* and *Main Currents of Marxism*.)

With this kind of background, it comes as no surprise, I trust, that I really like this book, and find objecting to what he actually proposes here highly wrong-headed. In what follows, I want to say a bit about "graphs" and a bit about "trees," and explain why this sounds so promising to me. I am not going to say anything about "maps," because I don't think I have anything to add to that discussion, but I will, for the sake of getting an M in there, end with some remarks on "materialism." At no point can I pretend to be competent to evaluate the originality of Moretti's work within literary scholarship, to say how much of a departure, say, the trees really are. In a feeble attempt to pretend that my price is higher than a weekend in California and a review copy, I will make some criticisms, most about tedious extra stuff I wish Moretti had also done. I'd like to think that what I say will also have some value for those who don't share my rather HAPHAZARD INTELLECTUAL TRAJECTORY, but my experience with trying to communicate across disciplines means I'll get a warm glow if I'm even comprehensible, never mind persuasive. I am accordingly very grateful to the Valve, and especially to Jonathan Goodwin, for letting someone with my credentials (viz., none) participate in this event.

## GRAPHS

### *Do* Genres Come in Bunches?

Moretti makes a very striking claim in his first chapter: that genres of novels appear together, in clusters, separated by about 25 years, and disappear together too. Looking at his graph, my eye agrees, but my eye also tells me that there are faces in clouds (the East African Plains Ape is an incorrigible pattern-finder), and probability theory tells me that purely random processes can produce a lot of apparent clustering and regularity. What reason is there to think that what looks like genres coming in clusters isn't just coincidence?

Let's be a little more precise about what we'd mean by "chance" and "coincidence" here. One natural possibility is that new genres appear at a constant rate over time, utterly independently of one another. Every year, then, there would be a constant probability of a new genre forming, but whether it did or not would have no bearing on whether the next year saw a new genre. This is our null model—the one that says what things should look like if we're just fooling ourselves, and there are no clusters. To get slightly technical, the intervals between genre-arrivals should have what's called a geometric distribution. Assuming, for the sake of argument, that that's true, we can use the average time between genre-appearances (3.44 years) to estimate the most likely value for the probability of a new genre appearing in any given year (about 29%).

Once we assume that the inter-arrival distribution is geometric and find the parameter, we can simulate from it, and get examples of what Moretti's graph would look like, if only chance were at play.

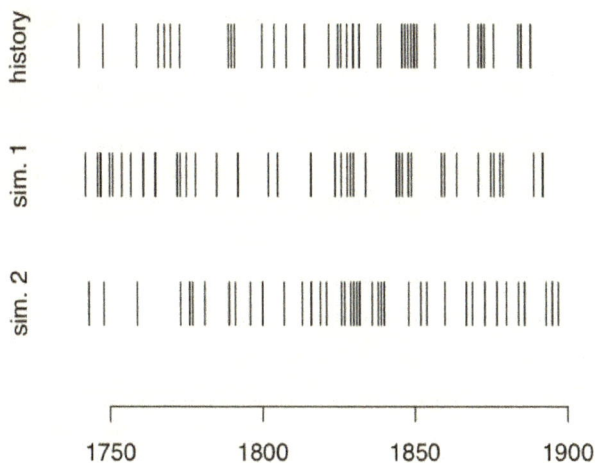

The top line shows the appearance dates of Moretti's 44 genres; the next two lines give the results of simulating from a model of uniform random appearance, with the same mean time between genres as the actual history.

Is there more clustering in reality than in the results of the null model? I couldn't say, by eye, but I don't have to. I can calculate the probability of generating Moretti's history from the null model: it's somewhat less than 1 in $10^{45}$. This in itself isn't decisive; any *particular history* becomes less and less probable as one considers longer and longer intervals of time (cue Stoppard), so we need to know what fraction of all histories of that length are at least that unlikely. I could work this out exactly, if I were willing to do some actual math, but I'm lazy, so I just had the computer simulate a million histories and evaluated all of their likelihoods. If the null model were actually true, we'd see histories like Moretti's only about 0.4% percent of the time.[1] So this is actually pretty good evidence that the null model is not true, and Moretti's history does show the kind of clustering he thinks it does.

Of course, this only underlines the question of *why* Moretti's data is clustered. I can think of a couple of deflating explanations (maybe the clusters match the periods more intensely scrutinized by historians; maybe they tend to adjust when they report genres appearing towards certain focal dates). Or it could be due to some sort of exogenous influence, from war, politics, economic shifts, etc. (I did not try removing the obviously topical genres, like Chartist novels, and repeating the analysis.) Or it could be due to some sort of endogenous mechanism within the system of literary production and consumption—generational turn-over of authors, of readers, of editors and publishers (suggested by my friend Bill Tozier). Or: maybe there's some space of things-people-like-in-novels, which the popular genres at any one time partition up in various ways; if one genre dies out or another appears, this might destabilize all the others as well. I don't think Moretti's time series, by itself, is enough to begin to let us decide among these mechanisms (some of which are compatible), but I do think it lets us see that *some* mechanism is called for.

Here is my first reproach: Moretti should have been the one to do this analysis, not me. If testing hypotheses is too banausic and mechanical for the pages of *New Left Review*, then it should either be in another article, or in the book. Moretti is a shrewd man, and in this case his intuitive analysis of the data was right, but there is no reason to rely on intuition alone for something like this. And, if one is going to go to the trouble to collect quantitative data, one ought to use it quantitatively. Mathematical abstraction (quantitative or otherwise) is not valuable for its own sake, but for the inferences it lets us make, when the proper tools are applied. In this case, those tools are pretty easy to bring to bear. They should be.

## Dissolving Genre History

Here is Moretti at the end of "Graphs":

> For most literary historians ... there is a categorical difference between 'the novel' and the various 'novelistic (sub)genres': the novel is, so to speak, the substance of the form, and deserves a full general theory; subgenres are more like accidents, and their study, however interesting, remains local in character, without real theoretical consequences. The forty-four genres of figure 9, however, suggest a different historical picture, where the novel does not develop as a single entity—where is 'the' novel, there?—but by periodically generating a whole set of genres, and then another, and another... Both synchronically and diachronically, in other words, the novel is the *system of its genres*: the whole diagram, not one privileged part of it. Some genres are morphologically more significant, of course, or more popular, or both—and we must account for this: but not by pretending that they are the only ones that exist. And instead, all great theories of the novel have precisely reduced the novel to one basic form only (realism, the dialogic, romance, meta-novels...); and if the reduction has given them their elegance and power, it has also erased nine tenths of literary history. Too much. (90)

On the one hand, this seems to me to be obviously correct. On the other hand, I wonder very much why Moretti stops here. If we look within any one of those forty-four genres, I think we have every reason to suppose that we'd find it composed, in its turn, of sub-genres, and so on, and ultimately of a shifting succession of individual texts. 'The' *Bildungsroman* (to pick one of the forty-four, not entirely at random) is a short-hand way of referring to the most common and enduring features of a historically-changing and always-various *population* of books, just as "the" bottle-nosed dolphin is an abbreviation for the leading tendencies of a certain population of organisms. What Moretti hints at, in the paragraph I quoted, is that "the" novel is itself a population, either of genres, or of texts structured into genres. But he doesn't say outright what seems very plain to me, and so I'd like to know why, and specifically whether he thinks it's actually wrong, or unhelpful.

> The assumptions of population thinking are diametrically opposed to those of the typologist. The populationist stresses the uniqueness of everything in the organic world. What is true for the human species—that no two individuals are alike—is equally true for all other species of animals and plants. Indeed, even the same individual changes continuously throughout its lifetime and when placed into different environments. All organisms and organic phenomena are composed of unique features and can be described collectively only in statistical terms. Individuals, or any kind of organic entities, form populations of which we can determine the arithmetic mean and the statistics of variation. Averages are merely statistical abstractions, only the individuals of which the populations are composed have reality. The ultimate conclusions of the population thinker

and of the typologist are precisely the opposite. For the typologist, the type (*eidos*) is real and the variation an illusion, while for the populationist the type (average) is an abstraction and only the variation is real. (Mayr, 84, quoting himself from a 1959 paper)

This makes salient the question of how we mark off different populations as distinct. The usual biological criterion is through common descent, and the possibility of inter-breeding—-Mayr's "biological species concept." (There is a vast controversial literature on the details.) Ruth Garrett Millikan has a closely related notion of "reproductively-established families," which doesn't lean so heavily on the details of biology, and which would seem to fit the case of genres of novels (Millikan, 1984). One could also define classes of texts purely morphologically, which might include many unrelated lineages (just as one might consider all streamlined marine predators which live in the water all the time, a class including dolphins, killer whales, sharks, tuna, ichthyosaurs, etc.). Just as such organic forms have appeared in several lineages, morphologically-defined categories could appear in multiple places and periods, the way novels arose, apparently quite independently, in both the Hellenistic world and in China (and elsewhere, for all I know). Historical populations, however, are unique.

## TREES

One could ... take evolutionary bibliography as the prototypical evolutionary science and think of biology in terms of bibliographic analogies...[2]

### The Cabinet of Horrors

People have generally sought to explain cultural change and cultural variation by supposing that culture is causally driven by something else (the climate, the social structure), or, more strongly, that it is *adapted* to something else, or, more strongly yet, that it functions adaptively for the benefit of something else (here social structure, or ruling classes, are favored as suspects over the climate). This has led to an awful lot of (if I may use the phrase) adaptationist just-so stories, and uncritical analogy-mongering on a level with the sort of thinking which leads rhinoceros horn to be prescribed for impotence. Jon Elster is worth quoting at some length:

> In his comments on the links among capitalism, Protestantism, and Catholicism Marx set a disastrous precedent for many later writers who have attempted to find "structural homologies" or "isomorphisms" (two fancy terms for "similarities") between economic structures and mental products. Because virtually any two entities can be said to resemble each other in some respect, this practice has no constraints other than the inventiveness of and ingenuity of the writer: There are no reality constraints and no reality control.
>
> Marx suggests two inconsistent lines of argument. One is that there is a strong connection between mercantilism and Protestantism, the other that there is an elective affinity between mercantilism and Catholicism. He was confused, apparently, by the fact that money has two distinct features that point to different religious modes. On the one hand, money (gold and silver), unlike credit, can be hoarded. Hoarding easily turns into an obsession, which is related to the fanatical self-denying practices of extreme Protestantism. On the other hand, money can be seen as the "incarnation" or "transubstantiation" of real wealth. In that sense the money fetishism associated with mercantilism is related to the specifically Catholic practice of investing relics and the like with supernatural significance. Both arguments are

asserted several times by Marx, each serving to show up the essential arbitrariness of the other. Later attempts to explain the theology of Port Royal, the philosophy of Descartes, or the physics of Newton in terms of similarities with the underlying economic structure are equally arbitrary. Like the analogies between societies and organisms that flourished around the turn of the century, they belong to the cabinet of horrors of scientific thought. Their common ancestor is the theory of "signs" that flourished in the century prior to the scientific revolution inaugurated by Galileo—the idea that there are natural, noncausal correspondences between different parts of the universe. What Keith Thomas refers to as the "short-lived union of science and magic" maintained a subterranean existence of which the doctrine of ideology, in one of its versions, has been one manifestation. (Elster, 183-184)

Even if we shutter and lock the Cabinet of Horrors, and go to look for explanations of trends in such cultural products as novels (which is, after all, what Moretti wants), I'm afraid we will find most of them in the capacious Closet of Mildly Appalling Objects. There is no shortage of attempts to give such changes meaning as signs of something else, some aspect of the social or economic structure, of the way we live now (or the way they lived then), but very, very few of them are convincing. In his great book on changing fashions, *A Matter of Taste*, the sociologist Stanley Lieberson looks at some of the reasons why these attempts at *ad hoc* explanation are so often bad. (He puts things more politely; I paraphrase.) First, the facts are often just screwy, both about the developments to be explained: non-existent trends, non-existent causes, weirdly mis-characterized trends, trends being explained by events which happened long after the former began, etc. (In fairness, such scholarly "misconstruction of reality"—*à la* Hamilton (1996)—is a lot more common than we academics like to think.) Second, the mechanism connecting the explanations to the *explananda* is left totally obscure. Third, no attempt is made to test the explanation, by checking that it can account for the magnitude of the observed change, by ruling out alternative explanations, or by much of anything else. The result is a steady stream of claims about how culture works which are advanced with what is, under the circumstances, an astonishing degree of assurance. Lieberson's book provides many fine examples of such cavalier just-so story-telling for names, the decline of hats, etc.[3]

Checking hypotheses about causation, and still more about adaptation, is really hard; with just one case, arguably hopeless. What you need is the ability to reliably detect departures from the hypothesis, if they are actually present— "power," in the statisticians' jargon. It is hard to get much power when $n=1$. If you want to claim that certain aspects of 19th century British novels were the way they were because those features fitted with ideologies of British imperialism— a fairly strong hypothesis about adaptation—I don't see how you can do it just by interpreting *Mansfield Park*, no matter how subtle and sophisticated your reading. On the other hand, if you look at lots of contemporary novels, and the ones which (say) depict Great Britain's relations with its colonies in the same way as *Mansfield Park* does are systematically more successful, on average, than those which depict it differently, well then I don't see how that couldn't be good news for your idea, though even that would really only be the beginning of backing it up.

Biologists *have* given a lot of thought to checking hypotheses about adaptation, and developed many means of doing so. *Mutatis mutandis*, many of these means could also be applied to literature, or other aspects of culture. Eric Rabkin,

Carl Simon and their collaborators have started doing just this with their Genre Evolution Project, looking at short stories from 20th century American science fiction, and no doubt there are others doing this kind of thing too.

One way of checking adaptive hypotheses, especially relevant here, is the "comparative method," or rather methods, which work much, much better when combined with good phylogenies. I think a literary historian who wants to study the evolution of genres and devices would be very well advised to look at the comparative methods biologists employ to study the evolution of qualitative characteristics of organisms. (The major issue would be that literary phylogenies will not be trees but more complicated lattices. But this is analogous to the effects of lateral gene transfer, common among bacteria, and so I'd suspect not only solvable but solved, someplace in the literature. Whether inheritance is by means of discrete-valued, particulate factors, i.e., genes, is not a crucial issue for such methods.) What I really want to see from Moretti (or *someone*) is a study along these lines of clues in the detective story; I'd be even more interested in one of free indirect discourse.

A crucial aspect of testing hypothesis about adaptation is a contrast with the outcome of a well-crafted *neutral* model— a way of saying what to expect if no adaptation were present, or not *that* adaptation anyway. These often have surprising consequences; for instance, neutral genetic drift will tend to fix some version of a gene in a given population, even if it confers no fitness advantage. (This is described in any book on population genetics.) So I wonder about things like whether we should expect, under a reasonable neutral model, that *some* formal device should become universal within a genre? If so, did clues take over detective stories any *faster* than neutrality would predict? (It's hard to imagine a successful genre where every story relies on confessions found by accident, but whether that's intrinsically weirder than actually existing detective stories, I can't say.)

The foregoing shouldn't be taken to mean that comparative literature should slavishly imitate comparative biology. There are people who have thought about the application of evolutionary ideas to social and cultural change in ways which are much more sophisticated about psychology, social organization and human interaction than (most) advocates of memetics; I am thinking particularly of DAVID HULL, W. G. Runciman, DAN SPERBER, Stephen Toulmin's great *The Collective Use and Evolution of Concepts*, and even the FRAGMENTARY MS. of Adam Westoby. As the economist RICHARD NELSON WRITES, we should expect our ideas of general evolution to change as we learn more about cultural evolution. We should also expect to have to develop different methods of data analysis. But, as always, we start with what we already know how to do.

## MATERIALISM

I share Moretti's hope for a "materialist sociology of literary form." I'd like a materialist sociology of culture generally. But I suspect it won't be able to do everything he wants it to.

When Moretti quotes D'ARCY THOMPSON on how the form of an object is a diagram of the forces which produced it, I'm happy to go along, and even happy to agree that this gives us some ability to work backwards, from form to force. But this sort of inverse problem generally doesn't have a unique solution, especially if some of the forces were transient and highly contingent ... Less metaphorically, something Lieberson argues very convincingly is that we often have to distinguish between the social forces causing there to be a change in some taste, and those which shape the *content* of the new taste. Often the latter mechanisms are more or less internal to the bit of culture in question, like ratcheting. Or:

culture doesn't have to express or reflect the social order. I suspect Moretti would be disappointed if this were the case for, say, genres of novels. Well, so would I. But this *needs to be checked*. One way would be to try to develop good neutral models, and see whether, and where, they break down.

Dan Sperber has a great essay, in *Explaining Culture*, on "How to be a genuine materialist in anthropology." He complains about treating Capital, the World-System, cultural symbol-systems, mentalities, etc. as reified causal forces, if not self-interested foresightful agents, forgetting that human history, society and culture are actually (if I may quote Marx and Engels): "real individuals, their activity and the conditions under which they live." It seems, at least to this interested outsider, that the study of literature in society also suffers from the ills Sperber diagnoses in anthropology. And I think what he advocates there should go here, too: give actual causal accounts of how macroscopic patterns emerge from the interaction of many *material* bodies (notably, people and books), of the sort we know to exist, endowed with the kinds of abilities we know them to have.

This commitment may sound harmless, because contentless, but it does actually have implications. It means that you have to do a lot of work to justify functionalist explanations (though it's not impossible. See Elster.) It should make you very dubious about ideal types (Mayer again. It should make you more interested in exploring variation, and not dismissing it. It should make you very dubious about "practices" and other shared mental objects, at least as ordinarily conceived (see Turner). And it suggests a lot of productive directions, investigating communication, cognition, and the collective patterns they produce.

In *Graphs, Maps, Trees*, as in his *Atlas*, Moretti is basically looking at the communication end of things. He doesn't say much about cognition, or individual thought more generally.

Elsewhere (see e.g. *Signs Taken for Wonders*) he has dabbled in psychoanalysis, but I hope that's past. A materialist theory of literary form will ultimately have to concern itself with the organic processes of reading and composition, but the way to do this is through empirical study of readers and writers, not more interpretation of texts, or armchair ruminations (whether those are on the primal scene, the environment of evolutionary adaptation, or conceptual blending). Of course literary scholars have been making stabs in this direction at least since I. A. Richards's *Practical Criticism*, but with the advent of cognitive psychology this can be done in a much more systematic way, combining modeling of cognition with experimental tests of the models.[4] Again, many people (e.g., JERRY HOBBS, HERBERT SIMON) have been proposing this for some little while, but it's only recently, with works like Bortolussi and DIXON's *Psychonarratology*, that people have begun to actually do it, taking the predictions of various theories of narrative, which say that changing stories in certain ways should affect readers' responses, and seeing whether THAT'S ACTUALLY RIGHT. This, and not desk-bound speculation about analogies, seems to me the proper way to start on a cognitive psychology of literature. It is obviously complementary to what Moretti wants to do, and (this is the sweet part) the two enquiries can be pursued in parallel; neither has to wait for the other.

One thing Moretti does *not* do, anywhere, is construct models linking individual behavior to aggregate patterns. Economists and sociologists already make such models, and anthropologists are starting to do so. It may be premature here, but ultimately it will be vital. If different social groups have different beliefs, is that because those beliefs express their relations to the mode of production, or is it because they tend to talk more with in the group than across group boundaries? Adaptationist theories of culture tend to go for the first choice, but WE DON'T REALLY KNOW whether the latter could account for the specific patterns of cultural difference and change that we see.

## How Not to Learn from the Natural Sciences

What I said above about not mindlessly imitating biology deserves some amplification.

Evolution ought to have a bad name in the study of literary history. Reading René Wellek's "The Concept of Evolution in Literary History" (or HIS ARTICLE for the Dictionary of the History of Ideas) is actually quite depressing. (The figures he discusses—not Wellek himself—bring to mind Kurt Vonnegut's line: "they deserved to fail, because they were all so stupid.") The many post-Darwinian ventures in this direction went, essentially, nowhere, at least as far as understanding literature better goes. It surely didn't help that their understandings of biological evolution were often very bad, generally some kind of Spencerian or even Lamarckian belief in tendencies of progressive development—perhaps inspiring, but hopelessly un-explanatory. (This has vitiated far too much evolutionary theorizing about social processes; cf. Toulmin's chapter 5.) As for the more recent wave, since the 1980s, the people who seem to think that literature exists because humanity craves dramatizations of Daly & Wilson's *Sex, Evolution and Behavior* drive me up the wall. (Their idea makes no sense even if you are very sympathetic to evolutionary psychology, which I AM.)

That said, this is not at all what Moretti is proposing, and I don't see the harm in trying to make this all fit together as another instance of a general explanatory pattern, alongside biological evolution, because they have similar causally-relevant features, and so similar mechanisms are at work. Many people have pointed out, in some detail, that explaining biological processes through the joint action of variation and selective transmission in populations is one instance of a general pattern of *historical* explanation; Toulmin is particularly clear on this.[5] There is a demography of businesses (Carroll & Hannan), of interest groups (Gray & Lowery) even of MEDIEVAL MANUSCRIPTS OF CLASSICAL WORKS (Cisne), and so why not one of literary texts? Inheriting discrete, particulate hereditary factors from a small, fixed number of immediate ancestors is not the *sine qua non* of this form of historical explanation, though the details of the process of inheritance will very strongly affect the character of the resulting dynamics. It might be that theories of literary change cast in this form are too complicated to be useful, or that we just don't know enough yet to find the useful ways to formulate them. But it wouldn't hurt to seriously try, and we'd learn a lot, no matter the eventual outcome.

**Varieties of Rational History**

One way to take the bit from Braudel about "a more rational history" that Moretti adopts as a motto is simply to hope that literary history will be a rational enterprise. There are various aspects to this—the accumulation of knowledge, a desire to give explanations, a realization that more than one explanation might be possible and a desire to check which one is right, and so on. To do all this, it's important to develop, use and refine reliable methods of inquiry—ones which are unlikely to lead you into error, and which tend to correct the errors they do make. You want to be able to persuade others, and you want to know that you're not *just* persuading yourself. As a statistician, my job is to help with the reliable-methods-of-inquiry bit, so it looms large for me. I think this is more or less what Moretti has in mind when he talks (elsewhere) about wanting "falsifiable" literary history—for ideas which have enough content that they can not only be communicated from one person to another (without tripping LIBERMAN'S

DETECTOR), but *checked*. Which said, I wish that here, as in his *Atlas*, Moretti *had* done a more systematic job of checking his conclusions. Would it be unfair to suggest that, while he sees the need for data analysis, it will be left to a successor generation to put it into routine practice?

If you want to say that asking literary history to be communicable, testable and reliable is asking it to be scientific and that's icky, well, it's a free country (at least for now). The more I think about what makes something a science, the less that seems like an important question. But whether something is a rational enterprise of inquiry matters. I'm sure it's possible to object to wanting history to be more rational in this sense, but I find that thought so alien and pointless I won't even try to engage it.

Another take on "rational history" is that the vast mass of details in small-scale history are essentially random, or, more exactly, the connections among them are as convoluted and involved as the details themselves. (This is one way to define randomness, mathematically.) But looking at larger scales, the randomness averages out, leaving regularities which are simpler and more nearly comprehensible by finite minds, and more reliable. As a statistical physicist and a statistican, I am the last to disagree: "In fact, all epistemological value of the theory of probability is based on this: that large-scale random phenomena in their collective action create strict, nonrandom regularity" (Gnedenko & Kolmogorov, 1). The small-scale details of literature and of human life have an intrinsic interest and value that is missing from the small-scale detail of molecular chaos, so there is certainly all the room in the world for what Moretti would like to do and close reading, *and* even essayistic appreciation. (But there is not, I am afraid, room enough in the world for Harold Bloom.) Whether there is room in an academy organized around the production of peer-reviewed research findings for all of them, is fortunately not a question I need to have an opinion on.

Finally, you might be tempted to go from the last sense of "rational" to supposing that large-scale history must be the working-out of some scheme which is "rational" in that it's really deterministic, or even teleological. This would be a mistake. It is not at all hard to give examples of stochastic processes that combine random evolution and feedback, which converge on very nice large-scale regularities, but *which* regularity they converge on is completely random and indeterminate.[6] Brian Arthur, among others, argues that processes like this are important in the evolution of technology. Is literature like that? I have no idea. But I don't see any reason it can't be, and this needs to be borne in mind.

## GO FISH

Let me close by quoting the same paragraph twice, once from the version in *NLR*, and then again from the closing pages of the book. In both cases, Moretti is enumerating themes which stretch across his chapters.

> First, a total indifference to the philosophizing that goes by the name of 'Theory' in literature departments. It is precisely *in the name of theoretical knowledge* that 'Theory' should be forgotten, and replaced with the extraordinary array of conceptual constructions, —theories, plural, and with a lower case 't'—developed by the natural and by the social sciences. 'Theories are nets', wrote Novalis, 'and only he who casts will catch'. Theories are nets, and we should learn to evaluate them for the empirical data they allow us to process and understand: for how they *concretely change the way we work*, rather than as ends in themselves. Theories are nets; and there are so many interesting creatures that await to be caught, if only we try. ("Trees," 63)

First of all, a somewhat pragmatic view of theoretical knowledge. 'Theories are nets', wrote Novalis, 'and only he who casts will catch'. Yes, theories are nets, and we should evaluate them, not as ends in themselves, but for how they *concretely change the way we work*: for how they allow us to enlarge the literary field, and re-design it in a better way, replacing the old, useless distinctions (high and low; canon and archive; this or that national literature...) with new temporal, spatial and morphological distinctions. (91)

Whether this pragmatic message is what Novalis meant, I have no idea; I only know the line because Popper used it as the epigraph for *The Logic of Scientific Discovery*. But that's what Popper meant by it, and I think it's right, and I LOOK FORWARD TO SEEING the coelocanths and tube worms and giant squid which will be brought up from the deeps in years to come.

originally posted, January 24, 2006

http://www.thevalve.org/go/valve/article/graphs_trees_materialism_fishing/

## Works Cited

Bortolussi, Marisa, and Peter Dixon. *Psychonarratology: Foundations for the Empirical Study of Literary Response*. Cambridge University Press, 2003.

Carroll, Glenn R., and Michael T. Hannan. *The Demography of Corporations and Industries*. Princeton University Press, 2004.

Cisne, John L. "How Science Survived: Medieval Manuscripts, Demography, and Classic Texts' Extinction", *Science*, vol. 307 (2005): 1305-1307.

Daly, Martin, and Margo Wilson. *Sex, Evolution and Behavior*. 2nd ed. Brooks Cole, 1983.

Deane, P. M. *The First Industrial Revolution*. 2nd ed. Cambridge University Press, 1980.

Elster, Jon. *An Introduction to Karl Marx*. Cambridge University Press, 1986.

Frawley, William. *Vygotsky and Cognitive Science: Language and the Unification of the Social and Computational Mind*. Harvard University Press, 1997.

Gnedenko, B. V., and A. N. Kolmogorov. *Limit Distributions for Sums of Independent Random Variables*, revised edition. Addison-Wesley, 1968.

Gray, Virginia, and David Lowery. *The Population Ecology of Interest Representation: Lobbying Communities in the American States*. U of Michigan Press, 2000.

Hamilton, Richard F. *The Social Misconstruction of Reality: Validity and Verification in the Scholarly Community*. Yale University Press, 1996.

David L. Hull, *Science as a Process: An Evolutionary Account of the Social and Conceptual Development of Science*. U of Chicago Press, 1988.

Lieberson, Stanley. *A Matter of Taste: How Names, Fashions, and Culture Change*. Yale University Press, 2000.

Lupia, Arthur, Mathew D. McCubbins, and Samuel L. Popkin. *Elements of Reason: Cognition, Choice, and the Bounds of Rationality*. Cambridge University Press, 2000.

Marx, Karl and Friedrich Engels. *The German Ideology: Parts I and III*. International Publishers, 1947.

Mayr, Ernst. *What Evolution Is*. Basic, 2002.

Millikan, Ruth Garret. *Language, Thought, and Other Biological Categories: New Foundations for Realism*. MIT Press, 1984.

Porter, Roy. *The Creation of the Modern World: The Untold Story of the British Enlightenment*. Norton, 2001.

Runciman, W.G. "The 'Triumph' of Capitalism as a Topic in the Theory of Social Selection", *New Left Review vol.* 210 (March-April 1994): 33-47.

—. *The Social Animal*. Harper Collins, 1998.

Sperber, Dan. *Explaining Culture: A Naturalistic Approach*. Wiley-Blackwell, 1996.

Thompson, E. P. *The Making of the English Working Class*. Peter Smith, 1999.

Toulmin, Stephen. *Human Understanding: Volume 1. General Introduction and Part I: Collective Use and Evolution of Concepts*. Princeton University Press, 1972.

Turner, Stephen. *The Social Theory of Practices: Tradition, Tacit Knowledge, and Presuppositions*. U of Chicago Press, 1994.

Winter, Sidney. "Natural Selection and Evolution." *The New Palgrave Dictionary of Economics*. eds. Eatwell, Milgate, & Newman, Palgrave (1987): 614-7.

## Notes

1   More on testing the null model of genre appearance, for those into that kind of thing: Really, of course, the most suitable null model for random appearance would be a continuous-time Poisson process. Since the data are discretized by years, however, I'm faking it by using a geometric distribution of inter-arrival intervals. (I also tried simulating from a Poisson process and then discretizing the result; the results weren't much different.) The only parameter of such a process is the mean inter-arrival time, or equivalently the "intensity," the probability per year of producing a new genre. Simple maximum likelihood estimation gives this as 0.2905405, which implies a log-likelihood for the original

data of -103.9498. To evaluate the significance, I generated 1,000,000 sample paths, of the same length as Moretti's, and then for each one re-estimated the intensity and used that to evaluate the log-likelihood. (This sort of "bootstrapping" should account for the fact that I fit that parameter to the data in the first place. It wouldn't be appropriate if, say, Moretti had advanced the conjecture that the mean inter-arrival time should be 10 years on *independent* grounds.) Of the 1,000,000 sample paths, only 3,802 had log-likelihoods as small or smaller than the original data. That is to say, if the null model were correct, we'd see results like this only about 0.38 percent of the time. So we can certainly reject the null model at the conventional 5 percent significance level, or even the 1 percent level, and in fact this is a considerably more severe test than that.

2   From Sydney Winter, who works out the analogy in some detail.

3   "Adventures of a Man of Science," Elif Batuman's wonderfully-titled review of *Graphs, Maps, Trees* in *n+1* magazine (January 6th, 2006), is a quite nice essay, but it also provides what looks like a typical example of the kind of mere plausibility I have in mind:

"Perhaps the Holmes stories are not half-baked versions of the "correct" mystery story, but a different kind of mystery story, wherein the nondecodability of clues is not a bug, but a feature. Conan Doyle was writing during the conquest of England by industry and rationalism; perhaps his readers wanted stories about the kinds of magic that are possible within the constraints of science. Holmes categorically rejects the supernatural, not in order to show that the new, rational rules preclude magic, but in order to show that you can still have magic even if you play by the rules. Decodable clues came a "generation" later, with Agatha Christie and the first World War, and became more rigorous after the second—by which time readers wanted to be reminded that the world was still rational." (146-147)

First of all, it seems bizarre to say that Britain was being conquered by "industry and rationalism" in the *1890s*, long after the scientific revolution, the Enlightenment (cf. Porter) the Industrial Revolution (cf. Deane)and all its social consequences (cf. Thompson), utilitarianism, etc. (Indeed, Mr. Lecky might want to have a few words ...) Second, Batuman gives us no reason to think that contemporary readers saw what Holmes did as (pardon the phrase) magic within the bounds of reason alone. Third, even if she were right about the social situation and the cultural product, the hypothesized causal connection is really just another arbitrary analogy, of the sort Elster complained about. Suppose Conan Doyle had been *better* about using decodable clues than Christie. Would it not then sound just as plausible to say this expresses the triumph of rationalism, followed by a post-war weakening? As it is, Batuman's account seems to appeal, implicitly, to a desire to hang on to older ways of thinking. Either the whole reading public of Britain in the 1890s is being treated, in a grossly anthropomorphic fashion, as a single *person*, with such a desire, or she is making a quite specific prediction about *which* readers Conan Doyle appealed to, one which does not seem especially plausible, though it might be tested. (It is utterly unclear *whose* purposes or needs are invokes by the in-order-to's—Conan Doyle's? his original readers'? society's?—but I fear the worst.)

Finally, no attempt is made to *check* that this is the source of the appeal, nor that the later strict decodability of clues really was caused by the World Wars, for the reasons given. I don't know enough to say that this suggestion is false, or that checking it would be impossible. I don't even want to suggest that a book review in a little magazine would be a good place to do such tests. But it doesn't seem to *worry* Batuman that there is no *support* for this idea (yet).—Let me repeat that I *like* the essay.

4   Incidentally, thinking that cognition is computational, and even that its computational architecture is strongly constrained by organically-evolved developmental processes, in no way commits one to denying that thought is also profoundly cultural and historical. Sperber is very good on this, but also see Frawley; or the papers collected in the Lupia, McCubbins, and Popkin volume.

5   Of course it isn't the only pattern of successful historical explanation. Even within the natural sciences, geology and astronomy provide very different ones.

6  More exactly, there are stochastic processes
("urn schemes") where the relative frequencies
of different outcomes are guaranteed to converge, with 100% probability, but the ratio at
which they converge is itself a random variable,
not determined by the initial set-up in any way.
The models of lock-in developed by Brian Arthur and his collaborators in the 1980s are urn
models, but actually less indeterministic than
the classical ones.

# ◣contributors

WILLIAM BENZON is an independent scholar and trumpeter. He is the author of *Beethoven's Anvil: Music in Mind and Culture* (Basic 2001). He blogs at the Valve, www.thevalve.org.

TIM BURKE is a Professor of History at Swarthmore College. He is the author of *Lifebuoy Men, Lux Women: Consumption, Commodification and Cleanliness in Modern Zimbabwe* (Duke UP 1996) and co-author of *Saturday Morning Fever: Growing Up With Cartoon Culture* (St. Martin's Press, 1998), as well as a variety of articles in African history, cultural studies and game studies. He blogs at Easily Distracted, weblogs.swarthmore.edu/burke.

Jenny Davidson teaches in the Department of English and Comparative Literature at Columbia University; her latest academic book is *Breeding: A Partial History of the Eighteenth Century* (Columbia UP 2008); and she blogs at Light Reading, jennydavidson.blogspot.com.

Ray Davis is a student in good standing and has completed all requirements except for dissertation. Advisors are welcome at pseudopodium.org.

Jonathan Goodwin is an Assistant Professor of English at the University of Louisiana, at Lafayette. He is working on a book about time in interwar British fiction.

Eric Hayot is an Associate Professor in the Department of Comparative Literature at Penn State University. His most recent book is *The Hypothetical Mandarin: Sympathy, Modernity, and Chinese Pain* (Oxford UP 2009)

**John Holbo** is an Associate Professor of Philosophy at the National University of Singapore and author of *Reason and Persuasion: Three Dialogues By Plato* (Pearson 2009). He blogs at the the Valve, at Crooked Timber, crookedtimber.org, and at John & Belle Have A Blog, examinedlife.typepad.com.

**Steven Berlin Johnson** is the bestselling author of seven books on science, culture, and technology, mostly recently *The Ghost Map, The Invention of Air,* and *Where Good Ideas Come From..* He is the co-founder of the web sites FEED, plastic.com, and outside.in.

**Matthew Kirschenbaum** is an Associate Professor in the Department of English at the University of Maryland and Associate Director of the Maryland Institute for Technology in the Humanities (MITH). His is the author of *Mechanisms: New Media and the Forensic Imagination* (MIT 2008).

**Sean McCann** is Professor of English and American Studies at Wesleyan University.

**Franco Moretti** teaches English and Comparative Literature at Stanford. In addition to *Graphs, Maps, Trees,* he has written four other books and edited, most recently, *The Novel* (Princeton 2006).

**Adam Roberts** is Professor of Nineteenth-century Literature at Royal Holloway, University of London. He is the author of a number of critical studied, including *The History of Science Fiction* (Palgrave 2006) as well as a dozen novels, all science fictional or thereabouts.

**Cosma Shalizi** is an Assistant Professor of Statistics at Carnegie Mellon University, and an external faculty member of the Santa Fe Institute. He blogs at http://bactra.org/weblog/.

9 7 8 1 6 0 2 3 5 2 0 5 6